EXCERCISE PAGES

Excercises and Tips
Day by Day

Fitness
& Relaxation

8 minutes per day to shape your body

28

day

fitness program

THORSTEN TSCHIRNER

BARNES
& NOBLE
BOOKS
NEW YORK

Contents

Your way to a top body

Your 4-Week-Program

1ST WEEK

2ND WEEK

Nutrition & Weight Loss

8

Your way to a top-body

8 Minute Training –
the fast way to the body you want

Do you run from one meeting to another, but there isn't any room in your tight schedule for a "real" workout? Have you given up your big fitness campaign after three trips to the gym? Or do you just need the final push to get you back on track?

For whatever reason you've been putting off going (back) into physical training, you'll find what you're looking for here: the quick daily work-out that will put your body into shape. It shows results, it has variety, and it fits easily into your schedule.

A university study has shown that only a brief daily workout can make you noticeably fitter. You only have to invest eight minutes a day! Where and when you do your express workout is up to you, although it should be mentioned right at the beginning that an active start to the day has a lot going for it (see from page 22). But most important of all is the regularity and intensity of your workouts.

Our eight minute workout has everything, since our training concept for each session includes

→ a warm-up to stimulate your circulation and metabolism,

→ strength training aimed at shaping specific muscle groups,

→ relaxation exercises at the end to round off the program.

HAVE A NEW AWARENESS OF YOUR BODY

It doesn't make much sense to try to change all your living habits from one day to the next – strict resolutions are almost always doomed to failure. That's why we're working through small, success-ful steps that will motivate you. The clear outline of the four-week plan ensures that you always see

Whether it's during a workout or a meal, as in all areas of life, (healthy) fun should be a priority.

TIP

Slim, fit, healthy — for that you don't need a strict diet. Start the program and follow some of the extra tips for nutrition and training. You'll be surprised at how fast you'll come closer to the body you want.

which step is coming up next. On each day of training you learn not only new exercises – you also get tips on how to finally get rid of excess pounds and build up toned muscle. The result: more energy, less stress, a totally new body feeling, and finally a great deal of fun and satisfaction.

THINGS ARE LOOKING BAD FOR THOSE EXCESS POUNDS

You know the exercise rule that says you can only lose fat through long endurance sessions done at a moderate pulse rate? In fact, this rule isn't entirely correct: what's really important is the fat burning factor of your activity. A look at your body's energy burning budget should make this clear.

It's a basic fact that you gain weight when you take in more energy – in the form of food calories – than you actually burn. It's simple arithmetic. But just how much energy do you need? Essentially, this is determined by two factors: basic energy consumption and active energy consumption.

By basic energy consumption we mean the calories that are burned when the body is at rest. This can be compared to a computer in standby mode. At 50 to 70 percent this makes up the lion's share of energy consumption. Anything that goes beyond that – running to the bus, cleaning the apartment, having sex, or of course doing sports – belongs in the category of active consumption, which depends on physical exertion.

As far as your metabolism is concerned, it really doesn't matter whether you burn calories through a round of jogging or through a weight lifting session. On the other hand, weight training makes muscles grow significantly stronger, and these are

your body's fat burning furnaces. The more you build them up, the more effectively you'll be able in the long run to get rid of the pounds on your hips and belly.

Exercise with results...

So the great thing about this is that you benefit twice from the eight minute workout: once from the workout itself, when a whole load of calories is burned, and then again afterwards when the fat-burning after-effect works on those excess pounds.

Even if it's mostly carbohydrates that are being used up during the relatively short eight minute workout time, your metabolism is still running at a high speed long after the power session. This means that any carbohydrates that you now fill up on go directly to the empty reserves in your muscles and subsequently can't be transformed into fat sitting on your stomach. And since, thanks to increased muscle growth, you're also burning more energy at rest, at the same time you're also burning fat while you sleep, without any effort! ■

Your body thanks you

→ **The best thing about regular workouts:** You don't burn extra calories only during physical exertion. With each extra pound of muscle your basic energy consumption at rest rises by another 100 calories a day. That's already 700 calories a week that you don't have to work off through physical activity.

→ **The kick you get from the eight minute workout** comes from the regular push that's given to your metabolism. And this is in combination with muscle buildup and stretching. With this program you burn fat, store up strength, and build up toned muscle. And your muscles are worked so continuously and intensively that they can do only one thing: they have to grow.

Mini workouts
with maxi results

Eight minutes doesn't sound like much? It really depends: with the workout described on the following pages you won't waste a single second of your valuable time. All you need is eight free minutes, a small space, and a pair of handweights (see box on the right).

How does this fast-paced program work? Very simply – through super sets! We've taken the basic idea from professional athletes. It's quick, easy to adapt, and at the same time highly effective: you carry out two exercises consecutively without a break. Right after one muscle, let's say the biceps, is worked on, its direct complementary muscle (in this case the triceps), or muscle group, gets the same treatment.

Through alternating the exercises this way, the most important muscles in your body are trained evenly. The results of our program are thus based mainly on the intensity of the individual exercise

sessions (sets) and on the lack of breaks. And for that eight minutes are enough – guaranteed.

ALWAYS SOMETHING NEW

We know how you can get tired of the same routines. That's why every day there are new exercises that challenge your concentration and your body, and that work on different muscle groups. So boredom isn't an excuse anymore.

Another advantage: You give your muscles time to adjust to the stress of the previous day. That way while working out at high intensity you achieve an ideal balance of exertion and relaxation of the individual muscle groups – and you get the most from your workout in the least amount of time.

Successful training – a question of combinations

The program is divided into the following groups of exercises:

→ day 1: legs and buttocks
→ day 2: chest and back
→ day 3: shoulders and stomach
→ day 4: biceps and triceps

This mix of training elements lends variety to the workouts and ensures the quick build up of toned muscle. It's not until the fourth week, after you've already achieved tangible, visual results, that the program then becomes even more intense.

In the end phase you aim at improving your performance through exercises that work on several areas of your body simultaneously. In addition, elements of movement to improve your balance are integrated. That's because coordination and posture are so important in realizing the body you want.

MUSCLE ALARM: HOW MUSCLE ACHES ARE CREATED

There are many types of aches that can plague us. Here we're interested only in muscle aches. Contrary to what many people think, it doesn't come from excess lactic acid in the muscles. Instead, it's due to tiny tears in the muscle tissue, so-called micro-traumas. Aches usually occur two days after strenuous activity.

Aches are especially common after muscles are subjected to unusual stress, or when they have to do yielding, eccentric work. An example: after climbing long flights of stairs you feel tired, but your muscles don't ache. However, if you run down the stairs instead, you'll hardly be able to move your legs the next day.

It's sometimes tough getting out of bed the morning after a heavy workout: all your muscles ache, and something as simple as brushing your teeth can make your biceps sting. But your muscles don't have to hurt after a workout. With the right know-how you'll be back in shape in no time:

→ Work out regularly. That way even new training routines won't cause muscle aches so quickly.

→ Always make sure you carry out the exercises correctly during the workout.

→ When training increase first the range of movement, and then the intensity of the exercise.

→ Regenerative exercise, such as jogging.

→ A sauna, or alternating hot and cold baths with rosemary.

→ A light, stroking massage – no kneading! ■

The right weights – a buying guide

Which weights are right for you? How heavy should they be (more about that on page 10)? And what else should you look for in them? Here are some of the most important tips for trouble-free dumbbell shopping.

▣ **Gripping! Get a good grasp on your weights.**
In contrast to weights with smooth or plastic covered handles, weights with grooved or textured chrome handles have a firm grip even when things get hot, your hands are sweaty and the weights are heavy. A possible side-effect: calluses.

▣ **A heavy decision: weight plates**
Muscles increase in mass only when the resistance applied to them also increases. Since it's important to build up healthy muscle in small stages, a good set of dumbbells should above all give you the possibility to add weight gradually. Ideally a dumbbell has enough space for several (up to four) plates of different weight on each side. Some sets include three pairs of 1, 2.5, and 5 pound plates. Ask about individual plates if you need to buy more equipment.

▣ **A secure hold: the lock**
After you've gotten yourself a set of dumbbells with changeable weights (see above) it's worth taking a close look at the locks that come with it. A set collar with a star grip enables you to change plates quickly and securely, and this should be your first choice. The alternatives: collars with a hexagon socket (Allen wrench, a bit fiddly) or a spring clamp collar (sometimes this is unstable).

▣ **Something for the eye: a question of design**
The decision to buy dumbbells and plates of chrome or cast iron depends mainly on how much you're willing to dish out, although personal taste plays a part. The cast iron variety is as a rule cheaper than the chrome, but its black painted surface tends to flake off with time, something that could irritate the more style-conscious athlete.

The clock is ticking –
the eight minute workout

About to start! In the box on the next page you can read about how your daily training session is organized. Here are a few more tips for a successful eight minute workout.

Quality instead of quantity

Always try to be aware of the parts of your body that you want to work on at the time. Concentrate on the details of the exercise. Ask yourself, "Which muscle is working right now? What does it feel like? Should I keep my body tensed, or should I ease up during certain exercises?" This way you're not only making sure the movements are being carried out correctly, you're also increasing your awareness of your body.

Here's a tip: Try to imagine how your muscles work. Studies have proven that by making a mental picture of your actions you're stimulating your performance.

So how heavy is it going to be?

Choose weights that are just heavy enough to make you struggle a bit during the last two reps. When exercising without weights, continue as long as possible and don't stop as soon as the body part you're working on starts to feel exhausted. That stinging sensation in the muscles ensures maximum training results, but of course only when you have enough strength to carry out the exercise absolutely correctly.

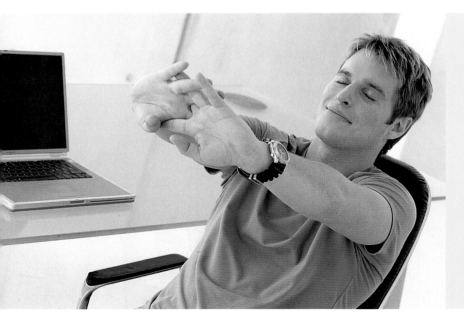

Feeling tense, stressed out, exhausted? With the eight minute program these problems will soon be a thing of the past.

TIP **Absolutely essential for the success** of your high-speed workout is the correct execution of each exercise. Only this way will you achieve optimal results and tight muscles. Slow, concentrated movements and a smooth technique are ideal.

Don't rush things

Just because your daily workout quota lasts only eight minutes doesn't mean you have to rush through the exercises. Take exactly the right amount of time for each movement. With dumbbell exercises, for example, that's two seconds to lift and two to four seconds to lower the weights. Only this way are you working through the strength of your muscles, and not through momentum. Also, when you lift weights too quickly you're risking injury to joints and ligaments.

Use your sense of perception

When performing an exercise use the greatest possible radius of movement so that your muscles are fully and correctly worked on. At the same time you should take care that the joints involved in the exercise aren't fully extended. This makes it easier on the joints and keeps muscle tension steady. Tip: From time to time check your movements in a mirror, or have your partner check them for you.

Always hold your breath? No way!

Even when the exertion makes you feel otherwise – when working out don't forget to continue breathing regularly! When you hold your breath you're doing what's called compressed breathing. This can raise your blood pressure, and in some cases can even be dangerous. So simply follow the golden rule: when flexing breathe in, when relaxing breathe out. Another plus: this breathing rhythm also makes it easier for you to relax mentally during the workout.

Let's stretch!

End your daily workout by stretching gently the muscle groups that have been worked on. Breathe regularly during these exercises and stretch the respective parts of the body far enough for you to feel a slight pulling sensation. Hold the final position steady for 10 to 12 seconds.

As a general rule: All strength and stretching exercises are always performed consecutively without a break on both sides of the body.

GO FOR IT!

Never forget: you made the right decision to start the eight minute workout. At the beginning of training you might now and then think that even these eight minutes aren't exactly a piece of cake. But then training is an (often exhausting) process and not a prize that you simply receive after a period of time.

So savor each successful step fully at the beginning – as a graduate of the four week program you'll soon have the new strength and energy to show just how good you are. A sure bet that our four week program will become your forty year plan. ■

The complete program

➔ **60 second cardio-moves as a warm-up (see starting page 18)**
First you get your body up to speed slowly with a gentle push of energy.

➔ **Two exercises each day for more muscle power**
40 to 60 seconds per set of each of the strengthening exercises. Beginners do two, advanced do three sets of each exercise.

➔ **To finish up: stretch**
30 to 60 seconds for an agreeable wellness stretching of the muscle groups which have just been worked on. Also good for overall relaxation.

Your 4-Week-Program

> "Even a journey of a thousand miles
> begins with the first step."
> (Zen saying)

1st Week

Are you going to make it? **Sure!** Because there's only one person who can answer for the success of our program: you yourself! If you're ready to make a commitment, you'll be rewarded at the end with a firm body. This book will help you: through our workout plan and many suggestions you'll already find it easier to achieve your goal.

The requirements for success are concentration when exercising and the determination to put what you read into action. Psychological tests have proven that prophecies can be self-fulfilling. So, if you're really convinced that you're going to stick it out, you will in fact make it. That's because all the processes in our bodies are closely connected to what's happening in our minds.

So also put your mental strength to work in successfully completing your daily program.

1ˢᵗ Day

Nice legs – tight buttocks

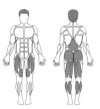

Let's move

Choose one of the cardio-moves (shown starting on page 18) to get warmed up in less than 60 seconds.

Let's work

1 EASY SQUAT

→ Stand with a chair behind you, your legs spread to shoulder width, with a dumbbell in each hand. Your arms are almost fully extended downwards.

→ Keeping your back straight, bend your knees far enough so that your buttocks are slightly touch-

ing the seat of the chair. If at first this exercise is too difficult, put a cushion or book on the chair so that your buttocks can reach it more easily.

→ Return to the starting position by nearly fully straightening your legs. Breathe evenly during this exercise: breathe in when descending, out when rising.

→ Do 2–3 sets of 10–15 reps.

 TIP

Read the exercise instructions thoroughly, even if you think you know the exercise. Often it's only a small difference in the details which makes for success.

Advanced: Start off the exercise with dumbbell knee bends.

→ In the starting position your legs are straight but not stretched out. Your feet are apart almost past hip width, and hip, knee and ankle form a straight line. Your arms are extended outwards with a weight in each hand. Pull your shoulders backwards and downwards, lift your chest, tense your stomach muscles.

→ Now bend the knees until your thighs are almost at 90 degrees. When doing this a slight forward tilt of the upper body is normal. Push your body upwards, your stomach remaining tense.

→ Do 2–3 sets of 15–20 reps.

POWER BUTT

→ Stand upright behind a chair with your legs apart to hip width. Support yourself by holding onto the back of the chair. Your upper body is straight, but tilted slightly forward.

→ With the weight of your body shifted onto your bent left leg, raise your right leg slightly and turn the knee slightly outwards.

→ Now raise your right leg backwards, without swinging, as high as possible. All this time your upper body remains tilted slightly forward and your back is straight.

→ Then lower the raised leg slowly forward. Change sides after each set. The range of motion in this exercise is rather limited; its intensity comes from your concentrated performance.

→ Do 2–3 sets of 15–20 reps.

TIP **When stretching also relax your mind –** free yourself from the usual competitiveness. Each person has his or her own stretch limit. Don't try to push it. Listen to your body. It knows what's best for you.

Let's stretch

BENT KNEE STRETCH

→ Stand facing a chair with your right leg stretched out, the heel resting on the seat. Your standing leg is slightly bent.

→ Bend your upper body slightly forward until you feel a slight pulling sensation in the back of the thigh. Keep your back straight while doing this.

→ Then repeat the same procedure with the other leg.

→ Hold on either side for 10-15 seconds.

A good start:
Cardio-moves to warm you up

Action, short and fast – even when the work-out's only eight minutes long, you should definitely warm up before any strenuous activity.

That way you'll gently get your body going. A warm-up prevents minor muscle pulls and other similar injuries, and it raises your working temperature. This makes all the muscles run more smoothly and effectively.

This type of preparation also gives you the opportunity to adjust mentally to the following exercises and to concentrate totally on your body.

So before each training session choose one of the following exercises (see next page). The warm-up set should last at least 30 to 60 seconds – it'll get you and your muscles fit for action.

BEFORE THINGS REALLY GET GOING

And here are a few tips before you seriously get down to business. As to equipment and place of exercise are concerned, you should observe the following points.

The floor under your feet

Avoid jumping and running on a concrete surface. A wooden floor is the best because it gives. In order to keep sliding to a minimum it's best to use a non-sliding runner (possibly with a rubber mat underneath) or an exercise mat over the wood.

The right shoes

Even if it strains relations with your downstairs neighbors – always wear sturdy training shoes that give you firm support and cushion the pressure on your ankle joints.

Make sure you have fresh air

When you're active you automatically breathe more deeply. Keep the window open while exercising, or air the room well before starting.

Always have enough room to move in

It's exactly during warm up that you get into motion, so reserve a place in your apartment where there's enough room – or where you can make room – to move your body.

Starting position

For all the exercises on this page start out in the following position: stand upright, with your chest raised and your shoulders pulled back and downwards.

It doesn't have to be boring!

After a while, when you've learned (only too well!) the different warm-ups, a session of rope skipping can help you get into the swing (see page 26).

Or you can drive away your inner demons with a quick round of shadowboxing (see page 27). ■

TIP **Don't measure your progress** by the scales. You can't tell from your weight whether you're succeeding. The only meaningful measure of your success is your fitness: that's why you should regularly take the test shown on page 126.

Let's get going

Cardio-moves to get you on the right track

MOVE NO. 1

→ March briskly on the spot. While doing this raise your knees high and move your slightly bent arms in sync. Roll your feet from the ball to the heel.

→ After 30 seconds, continue, now also rotating the shoulders forwards, then backwards, 10–20 times in each direction.

MOVE NO. 2

→ Run on the spot loosely for 30 seconds. Then spread your legs apart about the length of a step.

→ Continue for the next 30 seconds with your knees reaching to your elbows, alternating the left knee to the right elbow and vice versa.

MOVE NO. 3

→ Walk on the spot loosely for about 30 seconds. Then spread your feet to hip width, with the knees slightly bent. Your toes are facing out, your arms are stretched upwards.

→ Alternate bending each leg backwards, with the heel towards the buttocks. The right hand is lowered until it touches the left heel and vice versa.

MOVE NO. 4

→ Run on the spot. While doing this pull your knees upward forcefully, at first slowly, then somewhat faster. Gradually your arms are moving more energetically and finally your knees are reaching hip level.

→ Next round: now with your heels kicking towards your buttocks.

→ Lastly: Stretch your arms upwards and away from your body. When lowering them pull the elbows down behind your torso.

→ Attention: Keep your upper body in a vertical position during the entire exercise.

MOVE NO. 5

→ Starting from a standing position, jump and spread your legs to more than shoulder width. At the same time lift and join your arms over your head. Land first on the balls of your feet and roll back to the heels. Bring the feet back together with another jump.

→ After about 20 seconds bend the knees further with every jump until they're almost at an 80 degree angle.

→ For the last ten seconds go back to a looser, upright jump.

2nd Day

Quick workout
for the chest and back

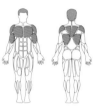

Let's move

Choose one of the cardio-moves (shown starting on page 18) to get warmed up in less than 60 seconds.

Let's work

1 STANDING BUTTERFLYS

→ Stand upright with your legs separated to shoulder width. You're holding a weight in each hand. Now lift the weights outwards from your sides to shoulder height.

→ In this position bend your elbows to a 90 degree angle in such a way that your upper arms are parallel to the floor and your lower arms are pointing upwards. Your arms are now in the so-called U position.

→ Now forcefully bring your arms together in a semi-circular motion to the front of your upper body. Make sure while doing this that you're always keeping your upper arms in a vertical position, and that your lower arms are at an angle during the entire exercise.

→ Concentrate on tensing your chest muscles once again just before the weights meet in front of your body. Only then do you return the arms, in one smooth motion, to the starting position.

→ Two to three sets of 10 to 15 reps.

3

body and the shoulder blades move towards each other. Concentrate on the tension in the upper back.

→ Stretch your arms out and upwards again, but without totally relaxing the tension. Now breathe in.

→ Two to three sets of 10 to 15 reps.

Let's stretch

3 CHEST STRETCH

→ First extend your arms straight out to the sides, then bend your upper arms upwards at a slight diagonal. The palms of your hands are facing your body. Contract the muscles in your back – from the lower spine to the back of the neck.

→ Now pull your elbows back and try to bring your shoulder blades together as close as possible. While stretching also try to pull the shoulders downwards.

→ Hold the stretched position for 10 to 15 seconds and repeat once or twice.

Careful: don't swing when carrying out movements. At any point you should be able to stop immediately.

2 SOFT PULL-UP

→ Stand upright with the legs separated at hip width and stretch your arms upwards. You're grasping in your hands at shoulder width the ends of a rolled up towel.

→ Now tug at either end of the towel as hard as you can. While maintaining maximum tension, pull the tightly stretched towel downwards behind your neck. Breathe out slowly while doing this. The elbows thus move backwards behind the

Eight minute training
according to your biorhythms

Owl or early bird: which training type are you? Can you hardly wait to jump out of bed in the morning? Then it's pretty clear you belong to the morning exercise crowd. But if you're a night owl and don't really get going until early evening then it's better to work out at that time. Each person has his or her own natural, fundamental rhythm, an interplay of active and restful periods. Practically all bodily functions follow this biological clock and adjust themselves during the course of the day. Learn to read your internal clock; it sets the pace for training and will tell you when it's time for a workout.

A FEW RULES – A LOT OF FEELING

Since each person functions differently, suggestions for the right workout time can only be approximate. Medically speaking, the best hours for physical performance are eight to ten in the morning and six to eight in the evening. That's when levels of strength and adrenaline are at their peak. There are in fact plenty of reasons for a quick workout in the morning (see box on the right), but in any case it's not advisable to push your body again just before you go to bed. That could disturb significantly your night's rest (see also from page 38).

Otherwise the rule is: Listen to your inner self. If you've just discovered your "best time" according to your daily rhythm, then try to stick to it during the four week program. Take your training seriously. Somebody who puts off his workout until "sometime today" usually ends up putting it off altogether.

So plan a fixed time for your workout the same way you plan any other important appointment. For example, you can treat yourself to an eight minute workout as a way of loosening up during

Greet the day with a smile – and an eight minute workout. It'll power you up for the new day, whether you're a late sleeper or an early starter.

TIP **For a good night** (see also page 39) get yourself moving after dinner. A brisk walk keeps fat-burning enzymes active through the night. You'll practically be slimming down in your sleep.

lunch break – or you can turn on the TV eight minutes later in the evening. In any case, it's ideal to get up a few minutes earlier in the morning: your body will gradually adjust to the added kick for the whole day.

Despite the advice about getting up early there's no need to worry. You don't have to start out cold in the morning. Right after waking up just stretch yourself out and tense your muscles, testing them. The result is that you breathe deeply, lungs and circulation pick up, muscles and ligaments expand. Then it's time to get up out of bed relaxed and ready to burn fat!

GO AHEAD! WORK UP A STORM!

We all know the feeling. After a few hours at the computer you've fallen into the midday slump – and your shoulder muscles have turned into jelly after this sitting marathon. Do you want to get out of this tired trap? Here's how:

→ Sit upright, raise your chest. Now place both hands on your shoulders: the right hand on the right shoulder, the left hand on the left one. Now with your elbows make small circles in the air. Gradually increase the speed and the radius of your movement to get things going.

→ After about 30 seconds gradually slow down the tempo so that you can change direction without a break.

→ Do this three to four times in each direction to stir things up. Already you're feeling fresh enough for the next meeting. ■

Five good reasons for an early start

After you wake up your body produces large quantities of hormones which induce alertness and euphoria. This makes you feel energetic and concentrated – just what you need for an active start to the day. And here's what you get:

→ **Morning activity is a real fat killer.** Researchers at Harvard University have found that the carbohydrate stocks in the muscles are nearly empty in the morning, causing the body to take the necessary fuel from stored fat reserves.

→ **Mornings are usually when you have time for yourself.** There are no appointments, no ringing telephones, no sudden obligations that might keep you from your workout. And: the earlier the hour, the fewer excuses you can think of. So your old "I forgot my gym bag" ego doesn't have a chance of fooling the new fitness-conscious you.

→ **People who work out in the morning hours** burn fat throughout the day – without any additional exertion. Just the short, fast cardio-set that starts off your workout (see page 19) peps up your circulation and metabolism, and burns fat. After the first minute or two you've already worked off 21 calories. And by the time you sit down at your office desk you've already burned up to 25 percent more calories than you would have without your morning workout.

→ **By exercising in the morning** you're building up right at the start of the day the strength and energy that enable you to work effectively and positively for the whole day. The reason? When you take advantage of the early hour you're rewarded first thing in the morning with a shot of the feel-good substance serotonin and the creativity hormone ACTH!

→ **You stay the course.** Researchers have found that 75 percent of women who train in the morning stick to their dumbbells. That's compared to only 25 percent of those who train evenings.

3rd Day

Attractive shoulders and a trim waistline

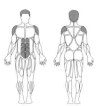

Let's move

Choose one of the cardio-moves (shown starting on page 18) to get warmed up in less than 60 seconds.

Let's work

1 LATERAL LIFTS

→ From a standing position step forward. Your chest is raised, your stomach muscles are tensed. You're holding a weight in each hand. Keep your slightly bent arms at thigh level with the hands facing inwards.

→ Now lift your arms to a horizontal position to the height of your shoulders. In the end position your wrists, elbows and shoulders form a horizontal line. Your hands are facing down and your arms remain at first slightly bent.

→ Then move your arms slowly back downwards while keeping the shoulder muscles constantly tensed.

→ Do two to three sets of 10 to 15 reps.

Advanced: You can increase the difficulty by extending your arms while doing this exercise.

2 CRUNCHES – A CLASSIC

→ Lie down comfortably on your back with your knees bent and your heels pressed to the floor. Stretch your arms out alongside your body.

→ Now flex your abdominals by moving your lower ribs towards your pelvis and your arms towards your shins. Your upper body thus moves upwards and forwards, and your shoulder blades rise from the floor. During this time, the head and neck remain at the same angle to the body.

→ Hold briefly, then tilt back and lift yourself again.

→ Two to three sets of 15 to 20 reps.

Let's stretch

TIP **Is this exercise too hard on the back of your neck?** Lie down on a large towel, grab the upper end with your hands and pull it tight. Now you can use the towel to support your head and take the stress off the back of your neck.

Advanced: Almost every abdominal exercise can be intensified by changing your position slightly, for instance the position of your arms: beginners do crunches with the arms stretched out along the body. More difficult: cross the arms on the chest. Next level: keep the hands to the sides of the head. Still too easy? Then stretch the arms out behind the head.

▣ FRONT TORSO EXTENSION

→ Lie on your back and stretch your arms as far as you can behind your head. Your legs are spread to about hip width, your feet hang out loosely.

→ Now stretch your body to its entire length. To obtain a greater extension you can place a rolled up towel under your lower back.

→ Hold the extension for 10 to 20 seconds. Repeat once or twice.

Variation: Do this stretch holding your hands, with the backs of the hands facing your head.

TIP **Become more aware of your body.** Stretch out both your left leg and your right arm completely at the same time. This way you're also stretching the lateral muscles of the torso. Then switch sides.

25

Warm-up variations
with jump rope and boxing gloves

The cool way to warm up: if you'd like to add some variety to your warm-up (see from page 18), why not try rope skipping or fitness boxing? Even if the last time you skipped rope was in your childhood you'll soon see how fast you can pick it up again. Boxing is just as enjoyable, and it's a real power cocktail: it's training for every muscle from the neck down to the heels. You can work off troubles and aggression, and replace them with a positive attitude.

GET A JUMP ON IT

You've always wanted to jump rope? Great. Rope jumping, or skipping, is becoming trendy again. Professional athletes have always sworn by it, and it's no wonder – always handy, and easy to use anywhere, the rope is hard to beat. With it you're benefiting all the muscle groups from the toes to the shoulders, with the thighs and buttocks especially getting a workout. And you're training your coordination – by jumping regularly, you become more agile and flexible in no time.

Basic Jump

→ Stand upright with your feet at hip width, parallel to each other. Place the tips of your feet on the middle of the – taut – jump rope and bring the handles up beneath your armpits. The elbows are close to the body, the underarms point outwards at a diagonal. The angle between the upper and lower arms should be at least 90 degrees. The hands are at about hip level, the knee and ankle joints slightly bent.

→ Now swing the rope loosely from wrists forward, helping only the first swing with a slight circular movement of the lower arms. Jump only high enough for the rope to pass right under your feet. This makes you land on the balls of your feet. When doing this the feet ease downwards but don't touch the floor. In order to cushion the impact, bend the knees slightly.

→ Jump for about one or two minutes.

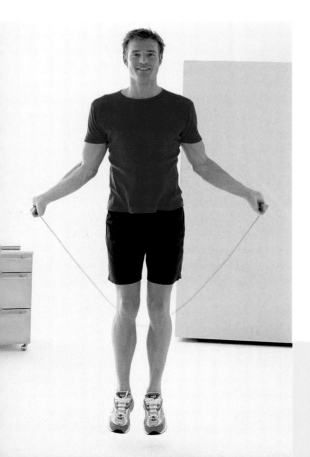

Jumping rope is fun and it keeps you fit – most people know that from their childhood.

WELCOME TO THE FIGHT CLUB

Sports researchers confirm the legendary effectiveness of this workout: what we call fitness boxing trains quickness, alertness, flexibility and balance. Also from a psychologist's point of view a boxer's training routine is an excellent outlet for stress. By letting your fists fly you can let off steam in a healthy way. Working out at the punching ball also makes you more self-confident. After a few punches you'll already feel better: your anger evaporates, your head feels clear, you're full of new energy. So get ready for the first round.

Shadow boxing as a warm-up

→ At first, skip around for two minutes like a boxer in the ring. Then begin with a round of shadow boxing against an imaginary opponent. Continue dancing light and loose on your feet – you're constantly in motion. Always think of new punching combinations to continue improving your awareness of your body and your ability to react. Steps, punches and kicks slowly blend into a flow of movement, stimulating your body. Don't forget that a shadow boxer is also up against an opponent, so don't let your guard down.

→ Do you have a bit more time? Then keep it up for another three minutes. Vary your leg speed and the frequency of punches as much as you can. It's OK if it gets a bit strenuous: with music from a favorite CD you'll work yourself into top shape.

Power Punch

→ In starting position you're holding your fists at cheekbone level in front of your face. Head, neck and back form a straight line. Distribute your body weight evenly between both legs, shifting most of it to the balls of your feet. The knees remain slightly bent throughout. If you're right-handed your starting position is with your left foot forward a foot's length.

→ Now twist your hips forward to the left side. Lift the right heel slightly. At the same time thrust the right foot forward. As you do this rotate your fist so that in the end position the back of the hand is facing upwards. Don't extend the elbow joint completely. The power for the punch should come mostly from the legs and hips.

→ Continue for at least a minute. ■

Power Punches are demanding for all muscles.
You will be full of new energy.

4th Day

Biceps, Triceps – getting your arms into top shape

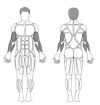

Let's move

Choose one of the cardio-moves (shown starting on page 18) to get warmed up in less than 60 seconds.

Let's work

1 CONCENTRATION CURLS

→ Sit on the front edge of a chair with your legs apart at slightly more than hip width. Keep your upper body straight while bending forward slightly. All this time your head, neck and back remain in a straight line. Support yourself with your left hand on your left thigh.

→ Place your right arm into position by resting the outside of the elbow on the inside of the right thigh. At first, let your right arm hang down loosely.

→ Without changing the position of the upper arm, now flex the elbow and, concentrating, bring the dumbbell up to the level of your collarbone. Then slowly lower it and repeat. Switch sides.

→ Do two to three sets of 10 to 15 reps for each arm.

Careful: Never bend your wrists back; during the entire exercise your lower arms form a straight line.

Advanced: In this variation you can give your biceps a real workout without risking injury. First continue carrying out the set until you can't do another rep, then take your left hand off your thigh and use it to support the right biceps for another two or three reps.

2 ONE-ARMED PUSHUPS

→ Lie down on your side. The arm under your body is curled up around your waist, and your free arm is propped up in front of you under breastbone level. Now press out the upper arm almost completely from the elbow joint. Your upper body is now lifted sideward.

→ Slowly lower yourself, but not fully – the arm in upper position should remain tensed. Then press upwards again, and when you've done this change sides.

→ Do two to three sets of 10 to 15 reps.

For your information: muscles not only strengthen you, they also slim you down. You could call them "make-up" for under your skin – and that goes for men as well as for women!

Let's stretch

TRICEPS EXTENSION

→ Standing upright, bend one arm backwards behind your head as far as it will go. Now with your other hand, press down carefully on the elbow.

→ Intensify the stretch by pressing the back of your head against the arm.

→ Slowly release the tension and change sides.

→ Hold the stretch for 10 to 15 seconds, then repeat once or twice.

It couldn't be more convenient: when you train at home you're not stuck to a gym's opening hours, you don't need to pack a bag, and you also save yourself gym fees.

On the go every day:
Eight tips for active living

Your new slogan: Don't spend a single day without moving it!

1 On your own two feet

You've always known it: it's better to go short distances on foot, than by car, bus or subway.

Go through a typical day in your head. It's not hard to find certain times when you can work on your body without having to put on a jogging suit. Put this knowledge into action: you can jog, bike, or rollerblade to work. Too much trouble? OK, then just get off the bus or subway a couple of stops early and walk the rest of the way.

2 Move it baby

Always keep moving. It doesn't matter if you set the right working pace by jiggling your feet loosely or casually snapping your fingers. By making these movements throughout the day you can increase calorie consumption by up to 20 percent.

And isometric exercises are especially discreet, since these involve muscle contractions that can't be noticed by other people. Whether you're on the phone or in a meeting, simply flex the buttocks for five seconds, relax, flex ... Repeat 10 to 15 times.

Get out of the cafeteria 3

Office, cafeteria, coffee corner, office – is this what your lunch break is like? Why don't you just take a walk for 15 minutes or so? You can switch off from work faster, and it's good for your figure, too.

4 Keep it personal

Thanks to telephones, faxes and email we don't have to budge from our desks in order to keep in touch with the world. This is fine if you want to reach a business colleague overseas. But do you really have to send an email to the office next door? Why don't you just walk over there – and if that very charming colleague has his or her office upstairs, all the better. You're working on your social graces as well as on your fitness.

5 Start climbing

You're not happy with the shape you're in and you still always take the elevator? Taking the stairs gives you a small training boost during the day. Besides which you're getting a great workout for the legs and buttocks which burns a whopping 144 calories in only fifteen minutes. So in the future keep it moving on the staircase. Don't miss a step in getting into the swing of things. However, you should cut down on the speed when going downstairs, in order to spare your knees the unnecessary stress.

6 For a strong midriff

Whether you're in your car, at your desk, or at the supermarket check-out: now and then simply pull in your abs towards your spine. When doing this keep breathing normally and try to keep the muscles contracted for about a minute.

7 Dancing fool

It's Sunday afternoon, you've slept well and are feeling oh-so relaxed. Could things get any better? Absolutely! Just slip a favorite CD into your stereo and start your own party. The longer, the better. And to really get things swinging, always keep your arms moving. This stimulates circulation and ends the weekend in an upbeat mood. Tip: in case your neighbors don't happen to share your taste in music, infrared earphones will help clear the atmosphere.

8 Give yourself a commercial break

On average, your TV set is turned on for about four hours a day. You should use this time to continue working on getting into shape. During commercials you should always slip in a few exercises from your eight minute workout. For roughly every 30 minutes of commercials you're burning 200 calories as well as building solid muscle.

5th Day

Nice legs – tight buttocks

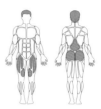

Let's move

Choose one of the cardio-moves (shown starting on page 18) to get warmed up in less than 60 seconds.

Let's work

1 SITTING LEG KICKS

→ Sit on the exercise mat with your slightly bent arms supporting your upper body from behind. Both feet are on the floor.

→ Now lift one leg a few inches from the floor and extend the leg as straight out as you can. Ideally, both knees are at the same level in the end position and you can feel the tension in your knee muscles quite distinctly. Hold this position briefly,

then slowly lower the leg without touching the floor.

→ Make sure that your back remains as straight as possible during the entire exercise.

→ Do two to three sets of 15 to 20 reps.

Advanced: Do the leg kicks now from a standing position.

→ Standing with your feet spread to hip width, lift your right leg. For support, use both hands to hold the thigh, which is kept in a horizontal position. Your standing leg is slightly bent, the upper body is leaning back a bit.

→ Now extend the right leg as straight out as you can. Your foot is relaxed.

→ Repeat 15 to 20 times, then do the same with the other leg.

BUTT LIFT

→ Lie down on your back. Your arms are lying next to your body with the hands pressed flat on the floor. Your knees are bent at a 90 degree angle. Lift your left foot and rest the ankle against the right knee. Tense your back and stomach muscles.

→ Now slowly raise your hips and lower back, keeping your buttocks tightly contracted, 5 to 10 inches off the floor. Both hips should remain elevated during the exercise.

→ Hold for the length of a long breath, then lower yourself at the same speed, without settling your hips onto the floor. Then lift again. Careful: don't push the hips out too far, the lower back shouldn't be curved in. If you can't manage at least ten reps, start with both feet on the floor.

→ Then switch sides.

→ Do two to three sets of 15 to 20 reps for each side.

Advanced: With one bent leg propped up, extend the other one straight out.

→ From this position now lift and lower your hips.

→ Do two to three sets of 15 to 20 reps.

Let's stretch

QUADRICEPS STRETCH

→ Lie on your right side with your right arm folded under your head and your right leg bent back slightly.

→ Now with your left hand grasp your left ankle and pull it back gently towards your buttocks. While doing this, tense your abs and keep your back straight. Don't twist your upper body while you're doing this.

→ Do the same now with the other side.

→ Hold the stretch for 10 to 15 seconds on either side and repeat once or twice.

Your office workout –
Keeping fit at work

An iron neck and rock solid back – sure you've heard of it. After a few hours in your office chair your neck is sore, your back is aching, your legs feel like lead, and your creativity is saying goodbye. Our bodies were simply not made for spending an entire day sitting at a desk! And then there's also the usual everyday stress: the trains are running late, the computer won't stop crashing, and the presentation has to be ready by noon. Situations like these affect your mood, and your posture also clearly suffers.

Quick office workout

Survival training for desk offenders

1 SHOW SOME BACKBONE

→ Sit upright with your abs tensed. Now tilt forwards with your back straight.

→ Draw your arms up and out so that your elbows are at a 90 degree angle.

→ Pulling your elbows and shoulder blades tightly together, twist your upper body as far as you can towards the left and then the right.

→ Do two sets of 12 to 15 reps. Each rep lasts six seconds.

2 FOR A FLAT STOMACH

→ Sit forward on the edge of a chair. Now lift your legs and lean your upper body backwards. Don't use your hands to do this.

→ Later you can intensify this exercise by pedaling in the air or crossing your legs.

→ Hold the position for 10 to 15 seconds. Repeat once.

A USEFUL TIP – SIT STRAIGHT

You can remedy a sad-looking "office body" through what we call active sitting. A rule of thumb: the height of your chair should always be adjusted so that the thigh and calf form a 90 degree angle.

Ideally, keep your sitting position as straight as you can. To do this, raise your chest and pull your shoulders backwards and downwards. Also important: at regular intervals throughout the workday shift your body position and always pay attention to your posture.

Try to slip in short exercise breaks as often as you can: for instance, you can spend some time making telephone calls on your feet and walk up and down a bit – it gives you a fitness boost (see also page 31). Also lay the down the receiver next to the phone now and then and treat yourself to an eight minute office workout. This short routine relaxes you, invigorates tired muscles, and stimulates not only your circulation, but also the productivity of your little gray cells. And the office workout includes only exercises that you can easily do at your workplace. ■

3 A SUPPLE BACK

→ From a sitting position, tense your stomach and back muscles. Now thrust your chest upwards, and at the same time stretch your back as far and as straight as you can.

→ Now place your lower left arm on your lower back. Grasp your left thigh with your right hand and pull the right shoulder as far as you can to the left. Twist your head and neck as far as you can in the same direction.

→ Hold for 10 to 15 minutes, then switch sides. Stretch each side twice.

4 STRETCH THE HIP MUSCLES

→ With your upper body upright, sit sideways on the chair so that you're able to stretch one leg backwards in front of the seat.

→ Now tilt back your pelvis. Your belly should also move back when you do this. Now push the chair slowly forwards a bit until you can feel the inner part of the outer thigh stretch.

→ Hold for 10 to 15 seconds, then switch sides. Stretch each side twice.

6th Day

Quick workout for chest & back

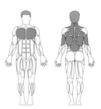

Let's move

Choose one of the cardio-moves (shown starting on page 18) to get warmed up in less than 60 seconds.

Let's work

1 DUMBBELL PRESS

→ Lie on your back on a mat. You're holding a weight in each hand. Now bend your legs up, with your feet flat on the floor.

→ If this position is at first too uncomfortable for you, you can lie more comfortably by supporting your head, neck and shoulders with a cushion or a rolled-up towel.

→ In starting position, your arms are extended to chest level and bent at a 90 degree angle, with your hands facing forwards. Now press and lift the weights in an arc to chest level above you. While doing this, twist your wrists inwards so that at the end of the movement the hands are facing each other. In end position, the elbows still remain slightly bent.

→ Check your movement – the dumbbells shouldn't hit against each other. Then slowly lower the dumbbells back down and repeat the entire movement.

→ Do two to three sets of 10 to 15 reps.

Advanced: You can make the exercise even more effective by consciously contracting your chest muscles as well.

2

TIP **Lateral pulls strengthen** primarily the muscles along the spine, in that way helping to prevent backache.

☐ LATERAL PULLS

→ Lie on your stomach with the tips of your feet pressing on the floor. Tense your buttocks and stomach. Your head is slightly raised but continuously forms a straight line with your spine. You are looking downwards. Stretch your arms out forward, and then rest them on the floor.

→ Now raise your arms and stretch one, then the other, forward. While one is stretching forward, bend the other one with the elbow moving towards your ribs. All this time keep your torso raised, but don't lift your upper body too much, and don't press your head to the back of your shoulders.

→ Concentrate on making a pulling movement; imagine yourself trying to pull a heavy object towards you.

→ Do two to three sets of 10 to 15 reps.

Advanced: Add dumbbells to the exercise. Often only the shaft of the dumbbell, without the weights, is enough to make the exercise more demanding.

Let's stretch

☐ SITTING LATERAL STRETCH

→ You're sitting with legs crossed on the floor. Extend your right leg out, with the knee facing

upwards. Rest your right hand on your right leg and extend your left arm upwards. Your stomach is tensed during this time.

→ Now bend your upper body slowly towards your right leg. Move your left arm along with it and stretch it out completely to the right.

→ Hold the extension on each side for 10 to 15 seconds, repeat once or twice.

3

Restful Sleep –
dream yourself fit

Sleep well last night? Did you sink into blissful slumber as soon as the light was switched off? Or were you still wide awake half an hour after going to bed? Unfortunately, for many that often seems to be the case. Sufficient nightly rest is actually just as important as eating, drinking, or exercise. After you've had enough restless nights even the fear of insomnia itself is enough to keep you from falling asleep. And after a period of time your body accumulates a sleep deficit that can't be made up, even by sleeping longer on weekends or free days.

WHAT HAPPENS WHEN YOU'RE ASLEEP

Happiness, so goes an old saying, depends on a good night's sleep. True! Because while we're dreaming away, hormones and enzymes are controlling the growth and repair processes in our bodies. Energy reserves are renewed, damaged cells in tissues are repaired. The immune system recovers from daily stresses.

What's more, a study carried out at the University of Chicago has shown that people who don't get enough sleep eventually gain weight. Essential metabolic processes are thrown off track by too little sleep. The awful consequences: sugar metabolism is disrupted and the body begins to put on fat deposits.

Lack of sleep also ensures that during the day we keep packing on the pounds. People who feel tired and lack drive believe they need energy. And the easiest way to stock up energy reserves is – that's right – by eating.

Time spent sleeping is not lost time: when you sleep you're renewing your body, mind and soul, making yourself fit for the new day.

> **TIP**
>
> **Free your subconscious** from everyday troubles and worries by writing about them before you go to sleep. That way, you can switch off more easily

JUST HOW MUCH SLEEP DO YOU NEED?

There's no single valid answer to this question. Some people manage with six hours of sleep a night, others need ten hours. Famous short sleepers such as Napoleon and Thomas Edison were satisfied with even less than six hours a night. So each person should first try to find out how many hours of sleep are ideal for him or her individually.

For your information: most people wake up seven to eight hours after going to bed. However, how long you sleep is not the most important thing: six hours of very sound sleep can make you more energetic than nine hours of tossing and turning. That's because it's only during deep sleep that the important metabolic processes needed for recuperation occur. It's during this time that the growth hormone which in adults supports the body's regeneration is released.

It's not important to notice as soon as the alarm clock goes off just how restful your sleep was. What's really important is that you should feel fit for the tasks of the day.

WHAT GRANDMA ALWAYS KNEW

Maybe you're still familiar with a few childhood tricks to help you fall asleep. For example: an evening bath relaxes muscles and has a soothing effect. Ideally, about two hours before going to bed you should get into the bathtub with the water at about 85 to 100 degrees. Do you often have cold feet? Then as soon as you've dried yourself off it's best to slip into a pair of thick socks.

Also good: warm milk and honey as a nightcap. Its effectiveness has been scientifically proven: this tasty mix ensures that large amounts of serotonin, the sleep hormone, reach the brain (see box on the right for more tips). ■

Trouble-free slumber

The good news for everybody who spends their nights tossing and turning: a few small tricks that will lure you into sleep.

➡ **Find your sleeping rhythm.** Establish a fixed time to go to bed and keep to it, even if that exciting movie on TV hasn't finished yet. Careful: it's especially at weekends that most people stay up late and sleep away the morning. When you do that, you're disturbing your sleeping pattern and you're getting a lot less rest than you'd like. It's better to maintain your normal sleeping habits.

➡ **Don't take naps if you're having problems sleeping.** Essentially, there's nothing wrong with having a midday nap; after all, humans have two periods of tiredness: one during the night, the other in the early afternoon. However, a siesta will take up part of your sleep quota. It's better to do without one if you're having difficulties sleeping.

➡ **Find the happy medium.** Give up on lavish late night dinners. But going to bed hungry won't help you sleep, either. So forget about extreme diets.

➡ **How about a nightcap?** Well, there's nothing wrong in that, as long as it's only the one glass of red wine. However, larger amounts of alcohol – starting from, let's say, half a bottle of wine – are taboo.

➡ **Schedule your workouts sensibly.** No more late-night sports – there should be a space of at least three hours between working out and going to bed (see also page 22).

➡ **Sleep with each other.** We mean what we're saying. After all, after a vigorous session of lovemaking between the sheets our hormones are serving us a pretty powerful sleeping potion.

➡ **Turn off the TV.** Put a stop to electro-smog and unplug the television and the radio in the evening. Even better, keep the TV completely out of the bedroom.

7th Day

Attractive shoulders and a trim waistline

Let's move

Choose one of the cardio-moves (shown starting on page 18) to get warmed up in less than 60 seconds.

Let's work

1 SHOULDER FLEX

→ Lie down firmly on your left side. Your left hand is propping up your head. In your right hand you are holding a weight and your arm is bent at a 90 degree angle. Your upper arms is resting on your right hip, and your lower arm is pointing downward.

→ Now pull your lower arm up to the maximum. Make sure that you're moving only your lower arm; the upper arm remains motionless.

→ Then switch sides and repeat the exercise with your left arm.

→ Do two to three sets of 10 to 15 reps each.

For your information: Even muscles which don't directly affect your appearance, such as those near the sensitive shoulder joint, have to be trained regularly in order to keep you in top form. This exercise, for example, strengthens the delicate shoulder joint.

TIP **Always curl your thumbs** completely around the weight and always keep your wrist straight. Otherwise you run the risk of spraining your wrist, even with light weights.

OBLIQUE CURLS

→ You're lying on your back with your left leg folded over your bent right leg. Extend your left arm out sideways and raise your right hand to the level of your temples.

→ Now contract your abdominals and bring your right shoulder to your left knee. When doing this, keep your back on the floor and your head straight. Make sure that you're moving not only your head and neck, but that you're also lifting your upper body and shoulder blades from the floor.

→ When contracting your stomach muscles always breathe out deliberately. This way you're getting the most out of this exercise.

→ Do two to three sets of 15 to 20 reps each side.

Advanced: To further increase the intensity, hold the end position for about two seconds.

Let's stretch

KNEE TWIST

→ Lie down relaxed on your back with your arms out sideways, at shoulder level, forming a U next to your head. Your feet are pulled up tightly to your buttocks, your knees tightly together.

→ Now tilt both knees to one side and have them touch the floor. At the same time twist your head in the opposite direction. Hold the position briefly. Try to breathe in deeply in the stretched side.

→ Then switch sides.

→ Hold the extension 10 to 15 seconds on each side and repeat once or twice.

TIP

When doing this exercise try not to raise your arms and shoulders from the floor.

"Not believing in your own body is the same
as not believing in yourself."
(Simone de Beauvoir)

2nd Week

Physical fitness is not a luxury. Much more than that, it's the engine that gives vitality to our lives — and that should be worth eight minutes a day to you!

A small psychological aid: picture yourself in different places and situations. The more realistic the picture, the greater your energy in realizing the goal. How are you going to look standing proud and upright? How do summer tops or tight T-shirts look over sleek, tight arms? Visualize the steps on the way to your goal. The best way to do this is through the pleasure principle: give your subconscious the right motivational kick by concentrating on the joys of living, the sensations you'll experience when you have a well-trained body and an active lifestyle.

And it's not just your body that you're getting into shape. By learning to surpass yourself, you're broadening your horizons and feeling fit for other newer, challenges. In this way, your training also strengthens your self-confidence, your patience and your determination to pull through in all areas of life.

8th Day

Biceps, Triceps – getting your arms into top shape

Let's move

Choose one of the cardio-moves (shown starting on page 18) to get warmed up in less than 60 seconds.

Let's work

1 ARM LIFT

→ You are standing upright with your chest raised. Pull your shoulders forcefully backwards and downwards, in this way stabilizing the entire

shoulder girdle. In starting position your knees are slightly bent and all your muscles, particularly in your stomach and buttocks, are tensed. If you want to be especially careful, stand with your back against the wall.

→ Hold the dumbbells to your sides at thigh level. Your hands are facing forwards. Your abdominals are tensed, your arms are almost totally extended. Careful: Your arms shouldn't be bent at too great an angle, and your elbows shouldn't be behind your body; otherwise the radius of movement for this exercise will be considerably shortened and the strain on the biceps will be much less intense.

→ Now bend your elbows and lift the weights towards your shoulders. Always lift the weights slowly and evenly, without jerking. Don't use your upper body to add momentum to the movement.

→ Do two to three sets of 10 to 15 reps.

Advanced: At the point of greatest tension hold the position for a few seconds, in order to increase the training effect.

2 STANDING KICK BACKS

→ Hold the weight in your right hand and take a wide step forward with your left leg.

→ Now bend your left leg far enough for you to be able to rest your lower left arm comfortably on your left thigh.

2

→ Lift your upper right arm so that it's parallel to the floor. The upper and lower arm form a 90 degree angle.

→ Now stretch your upper right arm backwards as far as you can. Hold briefly, then slowly bring it back down, until the elbow is at the same angle as before. Always keep your upper body straight and don't twist it to the side.

→ Slowly return your body to standing position. Take the dumbbell in your left hand and now work on the other side.

→ Do two to three sets of 10 to 15 reps.

Let's stretch

3 BICEPS AND WRIST FLEXOR EXTENSION

→ Extend an arm forward diagonally from your body, with the inner side of the lower arm facing up.

→ Now bend your hand downwards, using your other hand to pull the fingers gently towards you.

→ Hold the extension for 10 to 15 seconds, then switch sides. Repeat once or twice.

3

TIP

Avoid at all cost one of the most common mistakes when training your arms: getting other muscles in the shoulder area involved in this exercise. Move only the lower arms.

45

Bon Appétit!
Eating healthily and with gusto.

Starving yourself won't make you lose weight, and it won't make you fit. Here are eight tips for health-conscious and pleasurable eating.

1 Eat real food

Nowadays over 70 percent of our food has been modified through industrial processing. Artificial colors, flavors and preservatives, as well as thickeners and stabilizers make our food look appealing and prolong shelf life. However, with every bite of monotonous supermarket food our taste buds are constantly losing their sensitivity to subtle nuances. That's why you should try to buy as often as you can unprocessed foods, fresh herbs, and exotic spices. Also try to cook with the freshest ingredients you can get.

2 Let your body decide

Studies have shown: our bodies know exactly what they need. That means that when we listen to them we're automatically eating "right", so to speak. Physicians call this phenomenon somatic intelligence. So take the time to listen to your inner signals. You're worth the trouble; after all, your body isn't a garbage disposal.

3 Take your time

Slow down the pace when it comes to food. Choose your foods carefully, give yourself time for your meals. When you savor your food you also feel sated more quickly and you eat less. Chew every bite thoroughly. This also helps with your digestion by stimulating the fluids in your stomach, gall bladder and pancreas. A tip: try having music with your meals. Slow rhythms help you to slow down your chewing movements.

4 Gourmets enjoy every meal

Look forward to your meals. Try to eat in a quiet and relaxed atmosphere. Lay an elegant tablecloth, light the candles, add perhaps some flowers ... Stimulate all your senses: breathe in the aroma of the food before you slowly bring each morsel to your mouth. Lay down your knife and fork from time to time to lean back and relax.

5 Not when you're on the run

At lunchtime, you have some pizza to go, then after work something for the journey, and by the time you get home you're still starving. No wonder! Food that we eat when standing or walking doesn't register in our brains as a complete meal. The same is true for eating while reading or watching TV. The consequence: when eating "on the side" we lose control over the amounts of food and eat more than necessary – a calorie disaster. So get rid of any distractions before you eat.

6 Are you really hungry?

If you look inside yourself honestly, it's not hard to think of those situations when you've eaten without really being hungry – is that the case? We eat sometimes because it's time to, sometimes out of frustration, or to divert our minds from unpleasant tasks, or even occasionally to be polite. So ask yourself what's motivating you before you start eating . You'll learn to respond to your sense of hunger, and to spare yourself any unnecessary calories.

7 The old story of leaving the plate clean

Were you one of those children who had to leave their plates nice and clean? Then it's about time you freed yourself from your "good manners". Listen to your stomach when it feels full: at first force yourself to leave a little food on the plate uneaten. After a while you'll be able to recognize when your hunger has been satisfied.

8 Keep wet

Do you often feel tired and burned out? Maybe you're just not drinking enough! Drinking plenty of liquids is important for your well-being – after all, 70 percent of our bodies consists of water. You should be drinking at least 1.5 to 3 quarts a day. Water is the elixir of life: it transports important nutrients, and keeps the metabolism moving and those little gray cells on their toes.

9th Day

Nice legs – tight buttocks

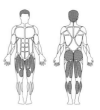

Let's move

Choose one of the cardio-moves (shown starting on page 18) to get warmed up in less than 60 seconds.

Let's work

1 LUNGES

→ Stand upright with your feet apart at a little more than hip width. Your stomach muscles are tensed. Fold your arms out in front of your body, so that each hand is touching the elbow of the opposite arm. If you had problems keeping balance while doing the short fitness check (see page 126), it's better to keep your arms spread out sideways at shoulder level.

→ Take a large step forward with your right leg, bringing your right thigh to an almost horizontal position. Make sure that your right knee doesn't jut out beyond your foot.

→ Return the extended leg to opening position and repeat the same procedure with the other leg.

→ Do two to three sets of 15-20 reps.

TIP **This exercise requires** a trained sense of balance. To get used to the sequence of movements, you should at first do this exercise without weights.

Advanced: You can do this exercise with weights in your hands. Your hands are facing inwards. Carry out the exercise as described on the left.

→ If you want to work more particularly and intensively on your leg and butt muscles, do the lunges using a step on the staircase or an other platform of similar height.

→ Do two to three sets of 15–20 reps per side.

▣ THIGH TONER

→ Lie down on your right side, with your head resting on your right arm, which is stretched out. Your left arm is supporting your chest. Bend your left leg forward and rest it on the floor in front of the right leg.

→ Now take the right, lower lying leg, off the floor and lift it as far as you can. Keep it extended with the foot parallel to the floor.

→ Then bring it slowly back down, without how-ever touching the floor. Then switch sides.

→ Do two to three sets of 15–20 reps.

Careful: Make sure to check repeatedly that you are lying in a straight position, and that your upper body is not swaying to the movement.

Advanced: If you like, you can also do this exer-cise standing in front of a wall. Move the leg that's being worked on slowly back and forth in front of your standing leg, but pay attention that your hips don't twist forwards and backwards. Adding ankle weights will make this even more demanding on your muscles. But you can also make it harder without extra equipment: press gently with your free hand against the thigh of the leg you're work-ing on.

Let's stretch

▣ ADDUCTOR STRETCH

→ From a standing position, spread your legs wide apart. Now shift your body weight onto your left leg and bend the knee. At the same time stretch your right leg, with the heel on the floor and the toes pointing upwards.

→ Now slide your butt backwards, tilting yourself slightly forward, with your back straight, and sup-port yourself by putting both hands on your left thigh.

→ Hold briefly, then switch sides.

→ Hold each stretch for 10 to 15 seconds and repeat once or twice.

TIP **If you want to extend** the stretch, simply move your legs further apart.

The Food Pyramid –
Tailoring your diet

Keep slim, but keep fit. There's plenty of information, tips, and rules on how to achieve that goal. The food pyramid on the next page will give you a quick overview of the most important food facts. It's based on the most current knowledge in nutritional science.

The base of the pyramid is made up of foodstuffs that are filling and that make you feel fit and healthy. At the top, on the tip, are the fattening foods. Eat according to the pyramid! The great thing about it is that you're spared any complicated nutritional arithmetic – you're working with portions.

TIPS FOR PLANNING YOUR DIET

Beginning with those foods which you can, and should, consume frequently, we give you now the "building blocks" of the pyramid:

❶ The broad foundation of the food pyramid is made up of whole-grain products, which deliver mostly carbohydrates as well as fiber. Thanks to them, you not only feel full longer, you also receive a good amount of vitamins and minerals. Combine them with the healthy unsaturated fats from vegetable oils (such as sunflower or olive oil).

❷ Don't hold back on the veggies. You can eat vegetables to your heart's content. When you eat plenty of vegetables, and a wide variety of them, you're strengthening your immune system against cancer, and against diseases of the heart and digestive tract. Two to three servings spread over the day delivers you a whole load of organic substances. One serving corresponds to one piece of fruit or a full cup of berries. At a pinch, you can substitute fresh fruit juice. Tip: The most important nutrients in fruits and vegetables are found directly beneath the skin, so don't peel them. Organic produce is therefore ideal in helping you avoid ingesting any possible residue from pesticides.

❸ Nuts and legumes are excellent sources of protein and they're also full of vitamins, minerals and trace elements. Nuts also contain a good deal of fat, but it's mostly of the healthy, unsaturated type (see page 55).

❹ There are clear distinctions among foods from animal sources. They are indeed rich in high-quality protein, but often also in saturated fats. That's why you should choose poultry: it's particularly low in fat. Fish contributes zinc and omega-3 fatty acids. And even eggs are healthier than you think: they are rich in unsaturated fats and vitamin B, without making your cholesterol level rise significantly.

❺ Get fit with milk – it's true. But two servings a day of milk or yogurt – in combination with other foods such as dark green vegetables – are all you need to supply you with high-quality protein and calcium.

❻ Candy and sweets, those classic fatteners, contain few nutrients and will make your blood sugar levels sky high. Up there at the tip of the pyramid they've got company: simple carbohydrates, such as those in pasta, which are very similar to sugar in their effects. Also in a leading position of notoriety are those products with a high content of saturated fats. All these foods should really not appear often on your menu. ∎

The Food Pyramid

EVERYTHING IS ALLOWED – IT'S HOW MUCH THAT COUNTS

Fresh fruit, vegetables and whole-grain products belong in a balanced diet, and so do animal products such as eggs, cheese and fish. They all make their contribution to healthy nutrition – even fats (see from page 54). The most important thing is always the right quantity. When planning your daily meals aim for variety, since each type of food has something particular to offer. And you should take advantage of them all!

6 Red meat, butter, also pasta, white bread, white rice, potatoes and candy: rarely.

5 Dairy products: once or twice daily

4 eggs, poultry, fish: up to twice a day

3 nuts and legumes: once to three times a day

2 vegetables: unlimited fruit: two to three times a day

1 whole-grain products: three to five times a day Vegetable oils such as sunflower oil, olive oil, soybean oil: up to 30 percent of calorie intake

10th Day

Quick workout
for chest & back

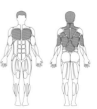

Let's move

Choose one of the cardio-moves (shown starting on page 18) to get warmed up in less than 60 seconds.

Let's work

☐ OFFICE PUSH-UPS ON AN INCLINE

→ Place your hands at slightly more than shoulder width on the stable edge of a table. Now stretch your legs behind you so that your weight of your body is supported only by your hands and toes.

→ Now bend your arms and lower your upper body far enough for your chest almost to touch the edge of the table.

→ Important: keep your body in a straight line and avoid curving in your lower back. Your weight is evenly distributed between arms and toes. When pushing up don't extend your arms fully.

→ Do two to three sets of 10 to 15 reps.

Advanced: Try varying the position – that way you can shift the focus of this exercise to the particular muscle groups involved. For example, if you want to train the pectorals intensively, spread your arms slightly past shoulder width. The closer your hands are to each other, the harder it is for the triceps.

Let's stretch

3 STANDING CHEST STRETCH

→ You're standing upright with your knees slightly bent. Deliberately relax the muscles in your neck and shoulders.

→ Now hold your hands behind your back and bring your arms slowly up. During the stretch keep your head straight and don't push your chin out. When breathing in, open out your chest forcefully and when breathing out, bring your arms up a bit further into a stretching position. Be careful that your lower back isn't hollow when doing this.

→ Hold the stretch for 10 to 15 seconds and repeat once or twice.

2 INCLINED ROWING IN SITTING POSITION

→ Sit on the edge of a chair, with a dumbbell in each hand. You're holding the weights with your slightly bent arms at the level of your calves, and your elbows are pointing outwards. Your feet are firmly placed at about hip level on the floor, the back of the legs form a right angle.

→ Now with your back straight and your abdominals tensed, tilt your upper body forward. Pull your elbows upwards as far as you can. Your shoulder blades will move towards each other when you do this. Always keep your head upright as a straight extension of your spine, and keep the stomach muscles tight.

→ Hold the end position briefly, then slowly lower the weights. The elbow joints remain bent throughout the entire exercise.

→ Do two to three sets of 10 to 15 reps.

Careful: During this exercise it's especially important that the upper arms are slidhtly spread out from the body. Only this way can you train effectively.

TIP
Think about it: regular training is the nicest gift you can give to your body.

Fat isn't always just fat

As a bicycle courier or an office worker – how active is your daily routine? How often do you really work up a sweat? That determines how much fat you need.

Help! Fat! – does the very word send a shiver down your spine? Fat is generally considered to be "unhealthy" and it "packs on the pounds". Unfairly so, since it's actually a marvelous supplier of those nutrients which protect nerves and organs. Several vitamins – A, D, E and K – can only be absorbed through the help of fat. Can you eat pork roast, then, with an absolutely untroubled conscience? Unfortunately not. As always, mindless indulgence is unacceptable. At nine calories per gram fat is at the top of the list of nutrients. In comparison, protein and carbohydrates have only four calories per gram. And because a heap of potatoes looks a lot heavier than the fat hidden away in food, we tend to underestimate the amount of calories we ingest as fat every day.

This fact is in itself not much of a problem for a bike courier. But most of us earn a living sitting at a desk. And: our energy needs may be lower for physically undemanding work, but the amount of nutrients the body needs remains the same. That means that even if you're sitting at the computer all day long you still need exactly the same amount of vitamins, minerals and essential fats as do your more physically active counterparts. Therefore, not only must you eat less in order to compensate for lower calorie consumption, you also have to find a way of planning your meals so that you're getting all the nutrients you need for healthy living. Instead of quantity it's quality that takes priority, and that goes for the quality of fat, too.

EAT FAT – THE RIGHT FAT

Nutritional fats are categorized not only as being animal or vegetable, but also according to their composition as saturated, monounsaturated, or polyunsaturated (see box at right). Unsaturated fatty acids, which are found in animal and vegetable fats, are of particularly high quality. It's important to note that our bodies cannot themselves produce unsaturated fats and thus depend on sufficient intake. Monounsaturated fats are also important for the body. On the other hand, saturated fats – found mostly in meat products – contribute only energy. Your body is able to produce

TIP **Fats differ** according to types of fatty acid.

Saturated fats: Too much can raise the risk of heart attacks and strokes. They are found mostly in sausages and cold cuts, meat, milk and cheese.

Monounsaturated fats: They keep cholesterol level low, and are found in olive, canola, and peanut oils.

Polyunsaturated fats: They keep fat levels in the blood low. They're found in fish, but also in thistle, sunflower, and walnut oils.

these fatty acids on its own, which is why extra body fat consists mostly of this type of fat.

Keeping your fat budget within limits

So you're not doing everything you can simply by eating less fat. You should consume fats in proportion to their different types. Nutrition experts recommend the following guidelines: a maximum of 30 percent of total calorie intake should come from fats. About a third of this daily supply should be in the form of polyunsaturated, at least a third in the form of monounsaturated, and a maximum of another third should be in the form of saturated fat.

So the idea is rather clear, but how to implement it? Very simply: choose vegetable products over animal products as much as you can. And watch out for hidden fat traps. Not just the well-known "classics" like butter, cream and cake, but also cheese, cold cuts, sauces, and sweet or salty snack foods.

You should reach instead for low-fat meat and dairy products. Anyhow, whole-grain products should be your first choice (see also page 50). They contain little fat, but are rich in vitamins, minerals and fiber. ■

Let fat help you keep fit

→ **It's variety that counts.** To ensure that you're getting the right amounts of the right fatty acids, it makes sense to use different oils when cooking. For example, in a salad dressing you can make mix sunflower, olive, and thistle oils together to get the greatest variety of nutrients from them.

→ **Keep a sharp eye out.** Try to do without processed hydrogenated fats – common in chips and salty snacks – and reduce your intake of animal fats (for example, high fat cheese or butter). Instead, consume more vegetable fats. Your body can use the vitamins they contain. As a spread, olive oil margarine or low-fat cream cheese are good alternatives.

→ **Be careful.** Buy oils in small quantities. Keep them well sealed and away from light sources. Some important fatty acids are very sensitive and are destroyed by improper or too lengthy storage.

→ **Use your sense of sight.** You don't have to give up on butter completely. But when you butter your toast, spread it on thinly enough to recognize the texture of the bread.

→ **Today we're having sushi!** The so-called omega-3 and omega-6 fatty acids found in fish are especially important. They protect blood vessels and the heart. The Japanese are not only champion sushi eaters, they're also the highest life expentancy in the world. Among Eskimos, who live almost exclusively off fish, heart attacks are also an exotic disease. That's reason enough to throw out a line once a week and haul in fish to your table.

→ **Techniques to keep you slim.** You can cut down by a good 75 percent on fat when preparing meals, assuming you use the right equipment. For example, there are pressure cookers, Dutch ovens, non-stick pans, steaming racks, and special wrappers such as baking bags. Meat, poultry, fish and vegetables cook in their own juices with little fat, and vitamins and minerals are better preserved.

11th Day

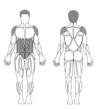

Attractive shoulders and a trim waistline

Let's move

Choose one of the cardio-moves (shown starting on page 18) to get warmed up in less than 60 seconds.

Let's work

1 FRONTAL RAISES

→ You're standing still with one foot forward, a weight in each hand, and your legs slightly bent

and spread at about shoulder width. Tense your the muscles in your stomach and buttocks, and keep your back straight.

→ Slowly raise an outstretched arm until the dumbbell is just below your eye level. Hold for a moment, then slowly and steadily bring your arm back down.

→ Avoid straining your shoulder joint and make sure you do this exercise slowly. It's safer, and in any case more effective in building muscle mass.

→ Repeat this movement, alternating the right and left arms.

→ Do two to three sets of 10 to 15 reps.

Careful: When doing frontal raises less experienced people tend to use their backs to add momentum – instead of using just muscle power – in helping to lift the weights. So it's better for beginners to do this exercise with their backs leaning against a wall.

TIP **Always remember** to use the strength of your muscles, without the help of gravity, to lower the dumbbells. You can check in the mirror to see how well you're performing the movements.

2

Let's stretch

3 PREVENTING A STIFF NECK

→ With one hand reach out over your head to the ear on the opposite side and pull your head sideward until you feel a gentle pulling sensation in your neck muscles.

→ Intensify the stretch carefully by extending the other arm near your body downwards and backwards.

→ Hold the stretch for 10 seconds on each side and do this once or twice.

Careful: When doing this exercise you must at all costs avoid any abrupt or fast movements.

Advanced: Grasp one dumbbell with both hands with your fingers intertwined around the shaft. Bring the weight upwards in front of your body.

→ Do two to three sets of 10 to 15 reps.

2 LATERAL BENDS

→ Stand up straight, with your legs spread at shoulder width. Tense your buttocks. Your right arm is extended downwards and you're holding a weight in your right hand. Your left hand is placed with the knuckles resting on your temple.

→ Now bend your upper body to the right as far as it will go, thus lowering the weight towards your knee. Don't twist your torso when doing this. The more you feel the muscles in the left side of your waist, the better. While doing this flex your abdominals forcefully.

→ Return to upright position and switch sides.

→ Do two to three sets of 10 to 15 reps.

3

TIP **During the stretching exercise** vary the motion, so that the individual muscle groups are trained at different intensity: one time turn your head towards the side being stretched, an other time turn it towards the other side.

Carbohydrates:
Starch, Sugar, Glycemics

Here you can go ahead and stuff yourself – as long as you choose the right type of carbohydrates. They deliver energy to the muscles, nerve cells and brain. And since your body can hardly store them, carbohydrates hold a special place among nutrients. Always welcome, they are absorbed before all other foods. But don't let that fool you. Just as with fats (see page 54), it's the "qualities inside" that make a difference with carbohydrates. Some of them will really give you a boost, others totally slow you down. Nutritionists speak of complex and simple carbohydrates.

NOW YOU CAN REALLY BE PICKY!

Complex carbohydrates consist of long chains of sugar molecules and are found mostly in wholegrain bread, brown rice, and vegetables. Since they have low amounts of fat and calories and usually contain high amounts of fiber, they keep our metabolism on its toes. That's because the sugar, in the form of starch, that makes up part of these molecules can be broken down only slowly, and by burning energy at that. So it takes some time before these long chains are split up. And that keeps levels of blood sugar and performance consistently high over a longer period of time.

In contrast, simple, short chained carbohydrates such as dextrose or fructose consist of single, or at most double, sugar molecules. They are found in candy and in processed foods. These have a negative effect on our metabolism: they cause a sudden

Sweet and yet healthy – it does exist! Simply help yourself to fresh fruit as often as possible.

Insulin is important in utilizing carbohydrates. It lowers the sugar level in blood, stimulates the buildup of fat deposits and keeps them from breaking down. That's because the quicker and higher blood sugar level rises, the more insulin is released and the more calories are turned into fat. The reason for this: too much insulin sends the body the message, "Store energy. Build up fat reserves."

rise in blood sugar levels. The body reacts immediately to this by causing the pancreas to increase secretions of insulin, the hormone that regulates blood sugar (see box above).

RECOGNIZE THE TRUE FAT MAKERS

After investigation of this mechanism nutritionists have created the glycemic index (GI). This indicates how different carbohydrates affect the blood sugar level. The higher the GI level of a particular food, the faster it makes the blood sugar level rise. Pure glucose has a GI of 100, foods with complex sugars and fiber have a value under 50.

However, the GI doesn't depend only on the amount of carbohydrates in blood and how fast they reach it. It also depends on how heavily the foods have been processed in the factory. That's because during processing long-chained carbohydrates are broken up, which results in them being absorbed at different rates in the digestive tract.

A good example of GI differences caused by industrial processing can be found in flour: the removal of the hull and germ from the wheat grain increases the shelf life of super-fine flour, but it loses practically all its vitamin and mineral content. At the same time its GI rises up to 90 – whole-wheat flour, by contrast, has a level of 50.

GLYCEMICALLY CORRECT EATING

As we've said before: you can eat as much as you want! But eat the right foods – the ones that will slim you down: healthy, long chained carbohydrates (see box below for some examples). The larger part of your carbohydrate intake should be made up of products with an index of under 51. On the other hand, avoid those foods with a high glycemic index, such as white flour, candy, and convenience foods.

But in case your blood sugar should happen to drop, it's better to reach for a piece of fruit. You're also better off eating whole-grain pasta instead of spaghetti, whole wheat instead of white flour, and rolled oats instead of corn flakes.

The best thing is to copy the box below and add the information to your shopping list, so it's always handy. ■

Eating with low GI levels

Foods with a GI of up to 50 will help you lose weight. Here are a few examples:

→ **Fruits and vegetables:**
Fresh fruit 10 to 30
Fresh vegetables about 15
Dried fruit or vegetables about 30

→ **Bread:**
Whole-wheat bread 50
Pumpernickel 40
Whole-wheat rye bread 40

→ **Side-dishes:**
Pasta made from cracked grain 30
Whole-grain pasta 40
Brown rice 50

→ **Dairy products:**
Plain yogurt 15
Skimmed milk 30
Most dairy products 35

source: healthy, vibrant, slim; Deutsche Ärzte-Verlag 2002

12th Day

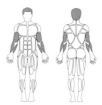

Biceps, Triceps – getting your arms into top shape

Let's move

Choose one of the cardio-moves (shown starting on page 18) to get warmed up in less than 60 seconds.

Let's work

1 CONCENTRATION CURLS / SITTING CURLS

→ Sit upright on a chair. Press your heels carefully into the floor, tense your abdominals and lift your chest. Holding weights, let your shoulders and arms hang down loosely at first, with your hands facing your body. When sitting you're not able to use your body to gain momentum. This helps you to execute this exercise perfectly.

→ Flex your biceps in order to bring the weights slowly up to shoulder level. At about thigh level start twisting your lower arms, so that in end position your hands are facing upwards. The advantage of this added motion: since rotating the lower arm is one of the two main functions of the biceps (along with the bending of the elbow), with this sequence of movements you're training your arms with extra intensity!

→ Now lower the dumbbells back into the starting position without swinging them.

→ Do two to three sets of 10 to 15 reps.

Careful: Keep your muscles tensed throughout the entire set. Also when lowering the weights back to the starting position, don't ease up!

2 CHAIR DIPS

→ Stand with your back to a chair. Support yourself with your hands placed palm down, fingers forward, on the seat of the chair. If this bothers your wrists, then use your fists instead for support. Your legs are slightly bent with your heels propped on the floor, your back is straight. In addition, pull your shoulder blades

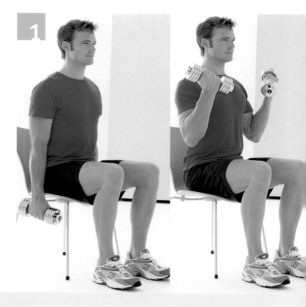

2

TIP **With chair dips you're hardening your triceps** – and it's only your arms that are moving. To achieve an optimal training pace, count to two when raising yourself, and count to four when descending.

together in order to help stabilize your upper body's posture.

→ Now bend your elbows until the upper and lower arms form a 90 degree angle. While lowering your body this way, you're keeping your buttocks as close to the chair as you can.

→ Slowly bring yourself back up. In the end position your arms should be nearly fully extended, but the elbows are not locked.

→ Do two to three sets of 10 to 15 reps.

Let's stretch

3 TRICEPS EXTENSION

→ Bring one arm behind your lower back. Bend the arm and bring it upwards as far as you can. In your other hand you're holding a towel.

TIP **You can make exercise much easier** on the joints by keeping them slightly bent when training them.

Bring the hand with the towel to the back of your neck.

→ Now grab the towel with the lower hand and pull down on it without letting go of the upper end. Hold the extension.

→ Loosen the tension and stretch the other side.

→ Hold the extension ten seconds on each side and repeat once or twice.

Protein –
great for building muscles

Each individual cell in our bodies consists of about 50 percent protein. In contrast to fat and carbohydrates, which serve as fuel for the body, proteins, the most important component of body cells, are our bodies' building materials. Some of them, such as collagen, are important for cell structure and give the body its particular shape. Others are responsible for muscle contraction and make it possible for you to move. In brief, for all processes connected with the growth of body tissue, including muscle growth, protein is essential.

In addition, almost every reaction of the body is linked to enzymes, which consist of protein. This is also true for fat reducers produced by the body, such as carnitine. Without protein numerous body functions, such as sleep, or digestion, or the menstrual cycle, would not be properly carried out. On top of that, this super substance makes you feel sated longer than fat and carbohydrates do, and in metabolizing it the body consumes more calories than for other foods.

FUEL FOR A TOP BODY

A protein-rich diet is also good for getting rid of body fat, since it stimulates the metabolism, helps break down fats, and regulates the appetite. The right amounts of protein in combination with physical training can also help you quickly obtain the body you want.

If your body receives too little protein over a longer period of time, sooner or later, body tissue will be affected. The body's own reserves will start to be consumed, and little by little you'll lose the

Yogurt and fresh fruit. With this dessert your body is getting a small protein boost, with vitamins, minerals and fiber added at no extra charge.

TIP

Smart combinations for trim muscles: Protein combinations of biologically high quality make it possible for you to get total nutrition without meat. Here are a few examples of foods that go well together:

Grains and legumes

Examples: pea dishes and bread, beans and corn tortillas, millet and chickpeas.

Grains and egg/dairy

Examples: whole grain cereals, bread and cheese, pancakes

Potatoes and egg/dairy

Examples: boiled (unpeeled) potatoes with curd cheese, potatoes and egg

have values between 80 and 90. When we consume meat and dairy products we're already taking in a relatively large amount of animal protein. These foods, however, contain besides protein many other components – such as saturated fats (see page 55) and purine – that have a negative effect on fat metabolism. But there are also protein powerhouses among vegetable foods: seeds, kernels, legumes, nuts, potatoes and grain products. Also, vegetable protein sources usually contain more of the healthy unsaturated fats and are cholesterol-free.

When skillfully combined, even low-protein vegetable foods can become sources of high-quality protein. These combinations supply valuable blends of proteins that the body is particularly well able to process. ■

muscle which you successfully built up. And that would be a pity!

Just how much protein do you need daily? The National Academy of Sciences recommends about 0.4 grams for every pound body weight. For somebody weighing 130 pounds that comes out to just under 2 ounces of protein per day. Protein cannot be stored by the body. It must be ingested anew every day. And, what counts isn't just the amount, but also the "quality" of the protein.

All proteins are made up of 20 amino acids, which are linked to each other in various combinations. Out of these 20 amino acids about half can be produced by the body itself. The remaining ones are essential, and they have to be sorted out from foods which are rich in protein.

A QUESTION OF QUALITY

The greater the similarity nutritional protein has to your body protein in its amino acid composition, the greater its suitability as a "growth food". This similarity is measured as a biological value: the higher it is, the easier it is for the body to transform nutritional protein into your body's own protein.

Pure protein has with the number 100 the highest value. Animal foods such as meat, fish and milk

Fit power through proteins

▶ **Do you treat yourself regularly** to protein shakes? Give them up! They don't make your body put on muscle any faster. Although protein is the most important building block for muscles, ingesting more of it doesn't automatically mean that you're going to get bigger muscles. That's because any superfluous protein is simply excreted from your system. With the recommended 0.4 grams of protein per pound bodyweight you're well taken care of. Distribute your intake throughout the day: your body can use small portions better.

▶ **Tryptophane is an especially important** protein building block. Lettuce, vegetables, milk, yogurt, fish, chicken and turkey are all rich in this amino acid. It helps ensure that our brains are getting enough serotonin. This is a hormone that enhances our mood and stimulates mental fitness.

▶ **Office workers** can also use a shot of protein to give them a boost. Lack of protein will quickly dull your performance at work. Here's a tip: have a glass of milk with pureed fruit as a between-meal snack . It'll pick you up in no time.

13th Day

Nice legs – tight buttocks

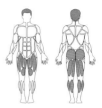

Let's move

Choose one of the cardio-moves (shown starting on page 18) to get warmed up in less than 60 seconds.

Let's work

1 SUMO KNEE BENDS

→ Spread your legs out wide, with your toes and knees facing out diagonally. Hold two weights in front of you at about the height of your lower ribs.

Lift your chest, and pull your shoulders forcefully backwards and downwards. You should feel distinctly the slight tension between your shoulder blades.

→ Now slowly bend your knees. If you can manage it, slowly lower your buttocks to below knee level. Otherwise stop before you've reached a 90 degree angle. While doing this tilt your upper body forward, the chest cage remaining raised.

→ Go slowly back to the starting position, but keep your the knees slightly bent.

→ Do two to three sets of 10 to 15 reps.

2 HIP EXTENSOR KICKS

→ Starting position is on all fours. You're supporting yourself on your forearms and knees, and your fingers are pointing forwards.

→ Take the left knee off the floor and raise it until the back and thigh are in a straight line. Also tense your stomach muscles.

→ The upper leg and lower leg are at a right angle throughout. Hold the tension, then lower. Now repeat the entire movement with the other leg.

→ Do two to three sets of 15 to 20 reps per side.

Advanced: From the same starting position pull one leg forward towards your chest.

→ Then bring the leg backwards until the hip is totally extended.

→ Do two to three sets of 10 to 15 reps.

Let's stretch

3 HAMSTRING EXTENSION

→ You're sitting on the floor with your legs stretched out. Lay a rolled up towel around the soles of your feet and grasp both ends. Pull on the towel until it's very tight.

TIP

Hip extensor kicks are one of the very best exercises for the buttocks.

→ Now use the towel to pull your upper body forward carefully towards your thighs. Your back remains straight and your chest is raised while you're doing this. During the extension continue breathing quietly and steadily.

→ Hold the extension for 10 to 15 seconds and repeat once or twice.

TIP

If you sit with your buttocks as close to the wall as possible you'll avoid unwanted wobbling.

Dietary Fiber –
anything but unimportant

Peels, seeds, tough rinds – many types of food contain indigestible components, so-called dietary fiber. We give the name fiber to a variety of carbohydrates and other compounds which for a long time were dismissed as unimportant. Two well-known examples of dietary fiber are cellulose and pectin. These are substances which make up the outer husk, framework, and support structures in fruits, vegetables and grains. They are also found in concentrated form in linseed and wheat or oat bran.

All these types of fiber are extremely important for our health, since they play a key roll in digestion and metabolism. And they start to show their positive effects the moment they reach your mouth: they require a greater amount of chewing, which gives the brain enough time to register food intake and turn off the sensation of hunger. For the same reason, circulation in the gums is stimulated.

Along with this, dietary fiber helps to regulate body weight: because it's hard to digest, it takes a longer time for hunger pangs to return after a fiber-rich meal. Foods rich in fiber expand in the stomach and stretch the stomach wall. The nerves there then send a message to the brain that you're full!

After a meal these healthy filling foods then ensure that the blood sugar level sinks very slowly and evenly. The pleasing result: insulin secretions are kept low (see page 59), you receive a steady supply of energy, and you stay "hunger-free" longer. In addition, fiber preserves the nutrients in food, thus ensuring the transmission of valuable other substances such as proteins and minerals, and brings your body into tip-top shape without making you spend a single calorie for it.

FIBER GUARANTEED TO MAKE YOU FEEL GOOD

In the stomach fiber regulates digestion and makes sure that your stomach doesn't begin to growl again so soon. This feeling of fullness lasts because fibers such as those found in grain hulls have the ability to absorb up to 200 times their own weight in water. This makes you want to drink, and your stomach fills up.

Tip: Best is the type of water-soluble fiber, for example in rolled oats, which soaks up especially large amounts of water, swells greatly, and thus stays longer in the stomach. Not least of all, fiber will calm down an irritated stomach by alleviating the effects of acid.

At the same time, undigested fiber also takes care of waste disposal. It binds toxins to the contents of the intestines and facilitates the excretion of digestive waste. In doing this it also gets rid of cholesterol-heavy bile and thus lowers blood cholesterol.

As it is, fiber makes everything work a little faster: fiber-rich meals stimulate the mobility of the digestive tract, and so prevent constipation, by "cleaning you out" after only 40 hours.

Afterwards, any remaining fiber from unexcreted matter is not absorbed by the intestines. That's because some fiber

TIP

And this is what a typical fiber-rich day could look like for you:

For breakfast fresh fruit with whole-grain cereal, yogurt, or on the side with bread.

As a snack fruit or a slice of bread with sliced cucumber, bell pepper, carrot or tomato.

For lunch a fresh salad and plenty of vegetables as the main course.

For dinner salad or uncooked vegetables with a cheese and herb dip.

tains more than white rice. That's another reason to switch to whole grains. You'll also find plenty of fiber in bran, whole-grain cereal, broccoli, red cabbage, Brussels sprouts, cauliflower, kohlrabi, and apples.

To make sure that nothing can go wrong, we've put together a small meal plan (see box at left). The basic rule is: eat fruits and vegetables five times a day, ideally three servings of vegetables and two servings of fruit, which adds up to about 600 grams. ■

– plant cell walls, to be exact – is broken down into short-chained fatty acids by intestinal bacteria. This way they help to prevent colon cancer.

AND HOW MUCH FIBER WOULD YOU LIKE?

You should consume about 30 grams of dietary fiber daily in order to obtain the greatest benefit. Unfortunately, very few people get this amount, although it's actually quite easy to obtain: about four slices of whole-grain bread and two apples or oranges, pears and carrots are enough to meet your needs.

Grains lose their cell walls during processing, which means that whole-wheat bread contains more fiber than white bread and brown rice con-

Have some top fiber foods!

These foods make it easy for you to load up on high-quality fiber:

Grain products:	
rye crisp bread	14.0
whole-wheat pasta without egg	9.1
whole-grain cookies	8.1
whole-grain cereal with dried fruit	8.0
whole-grain rye bread	7.7
whole-wheat bread	7.1
rolled oats	5.4
Vegetables and legumes:	
beans, navy	17.0
lentils	10.0
peas	4.3
cabbage	4.2
sweetcorn	3.7
broccoli	3.0
soybean sprouts	2.6
Fruit:	
figs, dried	9.6
dates, dried	9.2
prunes	9.0
raisins	5.4
kiwis	3.9
blackberries	3.2
bananas	3.1

(values in grams per 100 grams)

14th Day

Quick workout
for chest & back

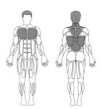

Let's move

Choose one of the cardio-moves (shown starting on page 18) to get warmed up in less than 60 seconds.

Let's work

1 LYING FLYS

→ Lie on your back on the exercise mat with a dumbbell in each hand. In this position you are holding your arms almost fully extended at mid-chest level, with the hands facing each other. When doing this exercise you can use a rolled up towel to support your head and neck.

→ Now move the dumbbells downwards in a wide arc. Your elbow joints remain slightly bent while you're doing this.

→ Just before your arms touch the floor, breathe out and at the same time lift the weights back to vertical position.

→ Do two to three sets of 10 to 15 reps.

Careful: During the entire exercise it's important that you don't change the angle of your elbow joints. Make sure that the motion comes from the shoulders. As soon as you bend your elbows the triceps start supporting the movement, and the chest muscles work less and are trained less effectively.

Advanced: You can make this exercise even more demanding when you overlap your arms at the end of the upward movement. In this way you're intensifying muscle contraction.

→ Do two to three sets of 10 to 15 reps.

2 REVERSE FLYS

→ You're holding a weight in each hand. Stand with one foot forward, your feet slightly over hip width. From this position go down on one knee by lowering yourself until the knee of the rear leg touches the mat and the front leg is bent at a 90 degree angle.

→ Then bend your upper body forward, keeping your chest raised.

→ Now lift your arms to the sides to shoulder level, in doing so bringing your shoulders together as far as you can. Throughout this your elbows remain slightly bent, head and back form a straight line, and you're looking down.

→ Do two to three sets of 10 to 15 reps.

Careful: It's very important that the wrists and lower arms form a straight line, and that they're not bent in or out.

Let's stretch:

3 BACK WELLNESS

→ Sit on the mat with your legs crossed loosely. Hold your hands with fingers intertwined and stretch out your arms at chest level in front of your upper body.

→ Tilt your hips forward, thus rounding out your back. Pull your arms forward as far as you can, so that your shoulder blades move apart.

 Do you often sit at your desk with a caved in chest and a rounded back? Then reverse flys are the right thing for you. This exercise compensates for bad sitting posture.

"Do not be afraid of progressing slowly,
        be afraid only of standing still."
(Chinese proverb)

3rd Week

Why on earth am I doing this? Be totally honest with your answer. Write it down on a piece of paper and tape it onto the door of the fridge, the bathroom mirror – it doesn't matter where. The main thing is, you have it in front of you several times during the day, so that whenever the slob inside you starts moaning again you have something to fight him with.

Another mood-killing thought: "other people can do it better". You're just making things harder for yourself. Don't pay too much attention to your weak points. Everybody starts off with their individual assumptions, their own strengths and weaknesses. That's why you should avoid comparisons which will only attract attention to the things about you that aren't so great. And you should have both feet firmly on the ground: when setting goals for yourself you have to know what's doable and what isn't. Set your goals high enough for you to just reach them when you make an effort.

15th Day

Attractive shoulders and a trim waistline

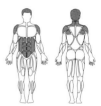

Let's move

Choose one of the cardio-moves (shown starting on page 18) to get warmed up in less than 60 seconds.

Let's work

1 SHOULDER ROTATIONS

→ You're standing with your legs apart at hip width and your chest raised, holding a weight in each hand.

→ Lift your arms out to the sides to shoulder level. Bend your arms at a right angle, so that your lower arms are pointing upwards at a vertical angle.

→ Now slowly rotate your lower arms downwards. Then lift again without swinging.

→ Do two to three sets of 10 to 15 reps.

Careful: When moving the lower arms keep the upper arms constantly in the same horizontal position.

2 HAND TO FOOT KNEE BENDS

→ You're lying on your back, with your shoulders slightly raised and your stomach tensed. Your arms are stretched out behind your head.

→ Now bend your right knee and bring it up to your stomach. At the same time move your left arm diagonally towards your right foot. In a smooth movement without pausing switch to the other side.

→ Do two to three sets of 10 to 15 reps.

Careful: The lower your extended leg is kept over the floor, the more intensive this exercise becomes, but also the more difficult it is to keep your lower back from curving in. If you notice that your lower back is arching from the floor, raise the legs higher. Or simply take a short break.

TIP
In order to avoid straining muscles, make sure your movements are done in an even rhythm.

Advanced: Place both hands behind your head. In doing this stretch your arms out wide. Then alternate moving each elbow to the opposite knee.

→ Do two to three sets of 10 to 15 reps.

TIP

Don't just carry out exercises mechanically – you should enjoy the feeling of power! It's incredibly motivating to feel the individual muscles working and to sense the potential that's within them.

Let's stretch

3 BELLY TIGHTENER

→ You're lying on your stomach on the mat, supporting yourself with your arms, which are bent and at about shoulder width in front of you.

→ Now slowly stretch out your arms. In doing this you're lifting your upper body, but your hips are still on the floor. Pull your shoulders downwards and backwards in order to intensify the extension.

→ Slowly release the tension and lay down your relaxed upper body on the mat again.

→ Hold the extension for 10 to 15 seconds and repeat once or twice.

Stress,
let it go!

Eight tips for a more relaxed day

1 Stress – often better than its reputation

Before you start badmouthing stress, remember this: in the past, stress has seen you through a number of tests, and it's also gotten you through some hard times. The stress reflex, which helped our ancestors to save their skins in very dangerous situations, is deeply anchored in our genetic makeup: all our organs are put into a state of alert, thus programming our bodies to attack or flee. Stress hormones are released, stimulating the heart and circulation. All essential organs – heart, brain and muscles – receive extra supplies of blood, and the entire mind and body are prepared for maximum performance.

2 Actions, not words

You can achieve a great deal by converting stress energy into actions. Positive stress, also called "eustress", can release an energy that's downright inspirational. However, any type of stress over a long period will make you ill. Instead of being more competitive, you become tired, lack concentration and be easily irritated ... Headaches, exhaustion and difficulty sleeping can be the physical effects, and apathy, anger, rage, and depression the psychological effects. Don't try to ignore stress: accept it, and use the power that it gives you.

3 Give your day a highlight!

Even if you've had a really tough day at work, when you get home don't just drop onto the sofa and fall asleep in front of the TV. It's better if you do something. After you've finished your eight minute workout, meet friends at the movies, club or sauna, or spend a nice evening with your family – it'll take the edge off of stress. Arrange times for feeling good and having fun as often as you can. And – make love. Sex is tremendously relaxing.

4 Let the animal out!

A stressed-out body thirsts for action and wants to strike out. Even if you think there's not a single spark left in you for working out, your body wants to get rid of its pent-up energy. That's another reason for working out every day, since the stress hormones adrenaline, noradrenaline and cortisole are broken down in no time.

5 Totally against stress

It's particularly during hectic periods that healthy eating is the key. Most important, make sure you're getting enough vitamin B1 and B6 (see starting on page 102). Also take care to get sufficient magnesium (see page 107). Alcohol and nicotine, at any rate, are to be avoided as much as possible during periods of stress. Even if it provides temporary satisfaction, you're still putting a strain on your body, and you'll have to pay for it later.

6 Do things in the right order

When things become hectic don't wring your hands in despair – get things moving, and in the right order. Take care of your work step by step, according to priority. You'll notice how stress diminishes even as you're sorting out your tasks according to their importance.

7 Giving too much isn't always worth it

Somebody who sets up a cot in his office doesn't always receive recognition for his efforts. That can be frustrating in the long run. Think about it: it's your life! And that's why it's extremely important that you don't lose sight of what's really important for you. Maybe you're wearing yourself out on something that means basically nothing to you. Give yourself regular periods of calm when you can be yourself and examine your goals.

8 Include breaks in your schedule

Always calculate more time than you think you'll need for planned activities. That way you'll give yourself periods of rest to collect new strength. If your schedule is already bursting at the seams, try starting the day half an hour earlier – and treat yourself now and then to a brief time out so that you can breathe deeply.

16th Day

Biceps, Triceps – getting your arms into top shape

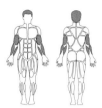

Let's move

Choose one of the cardio-moves (shown starting on page 18) to get warmed up in less than 60 seconds.

Let's work

1 HAMMER CURLS

→ Standing with one foot forward, pull your shoulders backwards and downwards. Your arms are along your sides, with a weight in each hand. Your hands are facing inwards with the thumbs on top.

→ Now begin bringing the weights up to your shoulders and then back down, without, however, extending them fully.

→ Do two to three sets of 10 to 15 reps.

Careful: During the entire exercise always keep your wrists in the same position: don't bend them! In order to work your biceps as intensively as possible, during the exercise keep your elbows to the sides of your torso without letting them swing back and forth. The easiest way to keep them like this is to maintain the tension at the beginning and at the end of every motion.

Advanced: You can increase the intensity even further by doing partial repetitions at the end of a set in order to tire out the muscles as fully as possible. Hold the maximum contraction for a few seconds before you lower the weight slowly back to the starting position.

→ Do two to three sets of 10 to 15 reps.

2 OVERHEAD TRICEPS STRETCH

→ You're sitting on a chair or standing with one foot slightly forward. Your buttocks are tensed, your stomach drawn in, and both arms are raised, one of them bent behind your neck.

TIP

This exercise is especially effective for the lower biceps area and the muscles of the lower arms.

→ After each set switch arms.
→ Do two to three sets of 10 to 15 reps per arm.

Careful: Never extend the arm fully, don't make the movements too wide, don't overstretch the joints. Otherwise there's a danger of straining your bones, tendons and ligaments.

Let's stretch

3 CHEST AND ARM STRETCH

→ From an all-fours position tilt your body a bit forward and stretch one arm as far as you can to the side, while you use the other arm to support yourself.
→ Now press the shoulder of the stretched arm to the floor at the same time as you pull up the shoulder of the supporting arm. The position of the thighs remains unchanged.
→ Hold the extension 10 to 15 seconds. Repeat once or twice on each side.

→ In the hand of the bent arm you're holding a weight at neck level; your elbow is pointing upwards. Use the other arm to support the weighted arm in its position.
→ Now breathe out, press the weight upwards, keeping your wrist straight, then lower it again.

TIP **You can also** carry out the triceps extension sitting on a chair.

Breathing is Life –
Energy from the Air

Breathe in, out, in again – we do this about 18 times a minute, 20,000 times a day, and 500,000 times a year. Totally automatically without thinking about it. It always works fine, even during sleep. But that's not quite the case: hectic activity, work stress and lack of exercise can make your breathing become shallow and fast, and your muscles cramp. This state of tenseness is registered by the brain. The result: mental and physical tension continue to rise. Under these conditions, air very often reaches only the upper parts of our lungs. This leads to decreased intake of oxygen, a rise in the amount of carbon dioxide in the blood – performance sinks, and you feel tired and burnt out.

To determine whether you're really breathing deeply or just gasping for air, you can do a simple test: lie down on your back and place a book on your stomach. Now breathe in slowly. What happens to the book? Actually, it should rise. If it moves downwards, along with your stomach, that means you're breathing not with your stomach, but with your chest.

You're able to breath deeply if your abdomen expands as you breathe in. Your diaphragm then has enough room to expand downwards. Breathing with your abdomen brings you inner calm and a feeling of well-being.

FILL UP ON ENERGY FROM THE AIR

But why is your personal well-being so closely connected to your breathing? Just what happens when you take a deep breath? Inhaled air flows past the larynx and the vocal chords into the lungs. There the oxygen travels into the alveoli, from there into the capillaries of the lungs, and finally enters the bloodstream.

The oxygen enriched blood flows into the left heart chambers and from there is pumped out into the entire body. When it arrives in body cells, oxygen works like fuel. It's only through oxygen that all the nutrients in food are burned, and thus converted into energy. The resulting energy affects your body temperature, your performance – your life.

OXYGEN, A MULTI-TALENTED PERFORMER

This special substance does even more for our bodies: this natural cell rejuvenator improves the immune system, speeds the transport of waste products, and helps with circulation problems and migraines. When you breathe out, you then expel carbon dioxide and other gases and dust particles which have been inhaled. Very often we remember to inhale deeply, but then don't pay attention to our exhaling. Yet this is important in helping the next inhaled breath to obtain enough fresh oxygen. Make sure you exhale forcefully, so that all the used air in your lungs is expelled.

You should also always maintain a natural breathing rhythm: in – out – breathing pause. Under stress we often forget the pause. The result: tension, which only increases the stress. Through consciously including pauses in your breathing you regain strength and repose.

The bottom line: deep breathing activates in our brains the substances which create a feeling of well-being, the so-called endorphins. It's no wonder that for centuries traditional health doctrines such as tai chi and yoga have used the power of breathing. The exercises on the right will help you gain new vitality even without yoga lessons. Go ahead and try them out right now. ■

Breathe easy!

Get more power through relaxed breathing exercises

1 TAKE A DEEP BREATH

→ You're lying on your back, with your hands next to your body and your eyes closed. Concentrate as you breathe deeply in and out three times. Count to five in your head each time you inhale and exhale.

→ After two minutes, rest both your hands on your chest and continue to concentrate on your breathing, so that your chest rises beneath your hands.

→ Rest your hands on your lower stomach, a bit below the navel. Breathe in deeply into your belly.

→ The right hand remains on the lower stomach, the left hand on the chest. Breathe slowly and evenly into both hands for about five minutes. Feel how the air spreads through the chest and stomach regions.

2 STOCK UP ON OXYGEN

→ You're sitting on the floor with your legs crossed and your spine upright. Rest the back of your left hand on your left knee. Your stomach is relaxed.

→ Now place your right thumb against the right nostril and your ring finger on your left nostril (see photo for position of the hand).

→ Now shut the left nostril and inhale very slowly through the right one. Hold your breath briefly before closing the right nostril and exhaling through the left one. Continue switching: inhale through the right and exhale through the left.

→ At first, count in your head to four, later to six if it's comfortable for you. The exercise should take two to three minutes.

3 BREATHE ENERGY

→ You're standing straight, with your knees slightly bent. Your mind is going through your body from head to foot.

→ Take two deep breaths. During the third breath lift your extended arms slowly over your head, with the palms of the hands facing inwards. Keep this position for as long as you can hold your breath. When exhaling, slowly lower your arms.

→ Repeat the entire exercise five times.

17th Day

Nice legs – tight buttocks

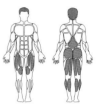

Let's move

Choose one of the cardio-moves (shown starting on page 18) to get warmed up in less than 60 seconds.

Let's work

1 DUMBBELL REAR LUNGES

→ From standing position with dumbbells in your hands step backwards with one leg. Lower the rear knee almost to the floor until the thigh of the front leg is parallel to the floor and the knee is vertical to the ankle. About two-thirds of your body weight should now be resting on your front leg. Throughout this your upper body remains upright and your stomach is tensed.

→ Now move out of this position, raising your hips and torso until the front knee is almost extended.

→ Then descend again immediately without a break. Switch legs after each set.

→ Do two to three sets of 10 to 20 reps per side.

2 GLUTES LIFT

→ Lie flat on your back and bend one leg up with the heel on the floor. Your arms are lying relaxed next to your body. Bend your other leg and bring it up towards your body.

→ Now lift your buttocks up from the mat until the thigh and torso form a straight line. Control

the tension in your buttock and torso muscles so that your hipbone doesn't tilt to the side.
→ Now slowly lower the buttocks a few inches and then lift them again into starting position. Inhale when descending and exhale when rising. Then switch legs and repeat everything.
→ Do two to three sets of 15 to 20 reps each side.

Advanced: Assume the same starting position as in the glutes lift, but now extend one leg upwards.
→ If you think you can handle more, instead of placing your heels on the floor in starting position for the glutes lift, put them on the seat of a chair.
→ Do two to three sets of 10 to 20 reps each side.

Let's stretch

3 BUTT STRETCH

→ Sit down on a chair, keeping your upper body straight and your shoulders relaxed. Now place one foot on the knee of the opposite leg.
→ Carefully press the top leg down, at the same time leaning your upper body forward. During this your back remains totally straight.

→ Carefully undo this position and slowly sit up straight again. Then switch the position of the legs.
→ Hold the extension on each side for 10 to 12 seconds and repeat once or twice.

Endurance Training –
a matter of the heart

How strong is your most important muscle? Even if you can hardly notice from the outside what sort of condition your heart is in, this muscle commands respect. It's the engine in our organism that handles the enormous workload of 41 million heartbeats a year. In doing so it pumps 2.5 million liters of blood ceaselessly and untiringly through our body. If it's ignored completely, however, it will exact a bitter revenge: should the engine start to splutter, you're in trouble.

That's reason enough to give it the attention it deserves through regular endurance training. Your heart muscle feels healthiest when you make demands on it. When it works efficiently, then your metabolism also functions perfectly, nutrients are processed optimally, the supply of oxygen to the lungs is just right, and the circulation and the immune system are strengthened – in short,

the entire body is in shape, and you don't get tired so quickly in everyday situations. The circulation in your skin improves and connective tissue stays firmer longer. You glow with vitality. To obtain this, it doesn't matter what kind of endurance training you do. The point is that you enjoy it. What's actually important is that in the future you work your heart once or twice a week for about half an hour.

The muscle you've built up from your eight minute workouts will also help you during endurance training. That's because the more mus-

Your pulse sets the right pace for you. With a pulse watch you always have it under control and you know if you're training at the right level of difficulty.

TIP

Forever young: By combining the eight minute workout now and then with the right heart-circulation training of your choice, you have a chance of staying 30 years old for the next 20 years!

cle you use, let's say, during power walking (see page 90), the more calories you burn. The fat-burning machine is running at full speed. With endurance training you raise your physical and mental limits. Endurance athletes are not only slimmer, they're also happier and healthier than couch potatoes.

In matters of stamina, as elsewhere, it's not the amount of training, but the quality of training that makes the difference. Punishing yourself until you're panting with your tongue hanging out won't get you anywhere, and is even unhealthy. When you train too hard the positive effects of endurance training are reversed. Circulation and the immune system are weakened through too much strain, and there's increased danger of injuring joints and tendons.

A rule of thumb for amateur athletes: after training you should feel so good that you want to continue.

KEEP BREATHING

While you're training, by keeping an eye on your heart rate (see box right) you're preventing overload and at the same time you're ensuring that your training leads to the desired results. Training according to your pulse rate gives you the big advantage of checking your progress, along with tailoring your workload. By observing your pulse you can see clearly the results of your training.

Here's how to measure your working pulse rate: interrupt your workout briefly for ten seconds. Now measure your pulse with your index and middle fingers, either on the inside of your wrist (the side towards the thumb), or on the carotid artery near the larynx. Multiply the number of pulse beats by six and you've got your current heart rate. It's easier to use a pulse watch. With this you can check your heart rate at any time while you're training. You also use the same method to measure your resting pulse, but this is done in the morning, about five minutes after waking up.

When we talk about exertion we generally differentiate between aerobic (the oxygen-rich zone under 80 percent of maximum heart rate) and anaerobic (the oxygen-poor zone of 80 to 100 percent of maximum heart rate) exertion. Training in the aerobic zone is especially ideal for beginners: heart, circulation and breathing function excellently, and the body gets all the oxygen it needs from breathing. You can of course spend some time exercising when you're almost out of breath, but your body benefits as little from exertion in the oxygen-poor zone as it does when you train sporadically or insufficiently. ■

How heated up should it get?

A lot of people miscalculate the pace, and most train too hard! This is how it should be done: Your individual workout zones are taken from your maximal heart rate (MHR) as a starting point. The basic formula is: 220 minus your age.

→ **You want to stabilize your health:**
Work out at 60 percent of your MHR. How do you feel? At ease – you can do even more.

→ **You want to activate your fat metabolism:**
60 to 70 percent of MHR is best. Can you talk while you're doing it? No problem.

→ **You'd like to improve your fitness:**
You should be at 70 to 80 of your MHR – bearable exertion.

→ **You want to increase your pace and stamina:**
Work out at 80 to 90 percent of MHR. Can you talk? Only if you have to.

18ᵗʰ Day

Quick workout
for chest & back

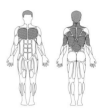

Let's move

Choose one of the cardio-moves (shown starting on page 18) to get warmed up in less than 60 seconds.

Let's work

1 EASY PUSH-UPS

→ This exercise is the perfect preparation for regular push-ups (see page 100). Lie face down and bend your knees by lifting your feet and shins off the floor. Cross your ankles and pull your heels slightly towards your buttocks. If you'd like, you can put a towel or cushion under your knees. Now extend your arms to use them to support your upper body.

→ Now slowly bend your arms until your upper body is almost touching the floor.
→ Then, in a smooth movement use your arms to push yourself up out of this position. While doing this your hands are apart at more than shoulder width.
→ Do two to three sets of 10 to 12 reps.

Advanced: Even in this position you can vary the degree of difficulty through a simple trick: the further your arms are from your knees, the more demanding the exercise becomes – and vice versa.

2 ON HANDS AND KNEES

→ You're lying face down on the mat. Raise yourself on all fours with your knees directly under your hips and your hands at shoulder level. Hold your head face down. Already from starting position try to keep your back straight and your stomach tensed. From this position stretch your right leg out behind you until it forms a straight line with your torso. At the same time extend your left arm forwards.

→ Hold for the length of a breath, then pull the elbow and knee towards each other diagonally under the body until they touch.

→ Do two to three sets of 10 to 15 reps per side.

Let's stretch

3 BACK ARCH

→ From an all fours position try to raise each individual vertebra in your back towards the ceiling. This results in the typically arched "cat's back". While doing this let your head hang down and tense your stomach muscles.

TIP
Give yourself periodic fitness checks (see page 126). They will motivate you, and they help even experienced athletes get the most from themselves.

→ In the opposing movement that follows, you then lower your chest as far down as you can while tilting your head carefully towards the back of your neck.

→ Make sure there is a smooth transition between all the movements and be conscious of the changing position of each vertebrae.

→ Hold the extension for 10 to 12 seconds and repeat the sequence once or twice.

Wellness Jogging:
getting into shape gently

How to find a place for training in even the most hectic schedule: For walking (see p. 90) and running you don't need expensive equipment or a health club. You can run anywhere and at any time. You can't beat the flexibility in setting up training times. But that's not all – regular jogging strengthens the heart and circulatory system, improves your feeling of well-being, and makes the brain work faster. The liver is six times more active in detoxifying. You can even run away easily from hunger, since the excess oxygen you get from moderate jogging makes you release more of the enzyme cholecystokinin. This is the substance that sends the message "I'm full!" to the brain. Before you start your first run through the park, forget about those people your age you've seen running past you with beet-red faces. Performance stress is completely unnecessary. Don't put yourself under pressure.

EASY AT THE START

When you start jogging you should be so relaxed that you're able to whistle a cheerful tune. If you

Running is a pleasurable activity. And if you can get someone to run with you, it's double the fun.

TIP
Your individual training pulse for wellness jogging:
Resting pulse + (220 − 3/4 your age − resting pulse) • 0.6

don't have the breath for it, then you're jogging too fast – along with about 80 percent of all joggers! Too fast a pace mainly puts your body under stress, making it difficult to increase its performance even slightly. All your effort would then be for nothing. Do you still remember the motto of our eight minute workout? Maximum results with the minimum of effort! Start out free and easy, without trying to break any records. The only important thing is pleasure in movement – the results will come later on their own.

You can turn jogging into a pleasant recreational activity simply by treating yourself as often as you can to a jogging tour through the nicest parts of your neighborhood. Physical activity should relax you, not build up extra stress. And don't let your first muscle aches discourage you, either. What's more important than anything else is that you've begun decisively to change your lifestyle and have already come a long way on your chosen path. Nothing and nobody can stop you now!

TOTALLY RELAXED WITH WELLNESS JOGGING

Periods of jogging and walking are combined with each other in this especially gentle variation on jogging. For example, you alternate between jogging for one minute and walking for the next.

An advantage: if you start out by jogging so much that you have to stop from exhaustion, then the walking break that follows is going to seem like a defeat. You can avoid this kind of frustration by planning your walking breaks in advance. Another benefit is that your muscles and joints are able to adjust gradually to increased demand and can also cushion, with the help of well padded running shoes, any possible stresses. ■

Keep it nice and easy

With the right technique and the perfect form you'll reach your goal relaxed.

→ **Make sure** that your torso is upright by lifting your chest, extending your back and keeping your head up high.

→ **Try to keep** your upper body still, moving only your shoulder joints. Also, your upper body should always be over your feet. Correct any possible shifts forward or backward.

→ **Shift your hips** slightly forward; otherwise it will be difficult for you to obtain a dynamic and efficient pace.

→ **Pay attention to your arms.** They should be bent with the elbows at about 90 degrees, and they should be swinging loosely at your sides without crossing in front of your body. A professional tip: swing more forcefully backwards than forwards.

→ **By using small steps** you'll get ahead without spending so much energy.

→ **Save valuable energy** by avoiding unnecessary bobbing up and down when running. The more you bounce, the less advantageous it is for forward movement. It takes a lot of energy to lift your body, then bring it forward and finally ease it down.

→ **While running make sure** you breathe with your stomach (see page 78). It's the better way to supply your body with oxygen.

→ **Don't look down.** Keep your head in such a position that you can see five to ten meters in front of you.

→ **Curl your fingers** into an open fist. Your thumbs are lying loosely on top. If you shut your hands tightly it only makes it easier for the neck muscles to cramp.

→ **The ideal spot** to land your feet when running is just in front of your body's center of gravity.

→ **Avoid** one of the most common mistakes: running with your legs too far apart. This makes the body sway. Instead, try to land your feet as parallel to each other as possible.

19th Day

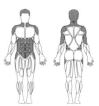

Attractive shoulders
and a trim waistline

Let's move

Choose one of the cardio-moves (shown starting on page 18) to get warmed up in less than 60 seconds.

Let's work

1 SHOULDER PRESS

→ You're standing with your arms stretched out from your sides and with a weight in each hand.

→ Now bring the weights up over you in an arc until your hands are nearly vertical to your shoulders.

→ Do two to three sets of 10 to 15 reps.

Careful: Keep your back straight throughout the entire movement. To monitor your performance better, you can do the exercise in front of a mirror.

Advanced: In starting position, rotate the lower arms so that the palms of the hands are facing each other. You can also do this exercise one arm at a time, alternating them.

2 SIDE HIP LIFTS

→ You're lying on the floor on your side, your upper body propped up on your lower left arm. Your fingers are pointing forward, the elbow is directly under the shoulder joint. Place your right hand loosely on your hip, and bend your legs back at a 90 degree angle so that the shins stabilize your position.

→ Lift your pelvis far enough for your entire body to form a straight line. Only the lower left arm and the left shin are touching the floor.

→ From this starting position, now push the pelvis upwards as far as you can. Your stomach is pulled in, your buttocks tensed.

→ Do two to three sets of 10 to 15 reps.

Let's stretch

3 SHOULDER STRETCH

→ Lift one arm to shoulder level and bend the elbow to a 90 degree angle.

→ Now bring the arm to the front of the body. Use your other hand to help you a bit by pressing against the elbow, thus moving the arm closer to the body. At the same time turn your head in the opposite direction.

To intensify the stretch, force your shoulders down. Then repeat the entire sequence, this time on the other side.

→ Hold the extension on each side for 10 seconds and repeat once or twice.

Careful: Always return to starting position slowly with your muscles tensed. Be careful that your hips don't tilt forwards or backwards.

Advanced: If you'd like to make things more difficult, carry out this exercise with your legs stretched out, supporting yourself with your feet instead of your knees. Or additionally you can raise your free leg slightly. But only well trained athletes will be able to manage it in this last position.

→ Do two to three sets of 10 to 15 reps.

TIP **You can, of course,** also modify the program according to your personal preferences. If, for example, a particular exercise doesn't appeal to you, you can simply switch it for one of your personal favorites. Just make sure that with this exercise you're training the same muscle group as was intended for the exercise you've left out.

Start walking –
slowly, but with power!

Power walking is a lot more than slow jogging. Here are six tips for more enjoyable walking.

2 Slowly, but powerfully

When you walk you're exercising continuously in the best health and fat-burning zone. You're getting your circulation running, your body is receiving the ideal amount of oxygen, thighs and buttocks are getting a thorough workout – great against cellulite. Walking gives a feeling of success quickly, and when it gets "too easy", you can simply shift seamlessly to wellness jogging (see from page 86). A flatter surface will guarantee you the best start. Walking through woods is ideal, but city parks or roads will also do.

1 Walk away your bad mood

Use this free and easy style of walking more often. You'll gently shape your body, drive away depression, and get into condition in an extremely effective way. At the beginning, fast walking might look like it takes getting used to, but – unlike jogging – doing it won't get you out of breath so quickly, and it's easy on the joints. The risk of injury is practically non-existent. In short, walking is the ideal (re-)introduction for anybody who hasn't been physically active for a long time.

3 The right walking technique

Stand up straight, with your stomach slightly tensed, your torso erect, your chest raised and your shoulders pulled down and back. Rock your feet from one end to the other. In contrast to jogging, one foot is always in contact with the ground and each step lands on the heel. You then consciously rock the foot forward and press down with your toes. Aim at using all the muscles in your calves. A good indication of the right walking technique is when you can hardly hear your steps. Your arms, bent at a right angle, swing along with your pace. Walk with fast, wide steps, and keep your knees slightly bent.

4 How fast do you want it?

As a general rule, it's how long you walk that makes for success, not how fast. You're exerting yourself at the right level when you feel better after walking than before. If you'd like to find out what your precise training pulse is, you can use special pulse formulas to calculate it.

5 You'd like to shift to high gear?

Then start by increasing your pace, and at the same time move your arms more energetically. Later you can make things more difficult on slightly hilly stretches by increasing the tempo a bit. You should not, however, add wrist or ankle weights. It takes only the wrong technique to increase the risk of injuries, especially for beginners.

6 An additional little workout

Draw an imaginary line down your walking route and follow it for about 500 meters. Land each foot in front of the other on the line as precisely as you can. Or try walking cross-country more often. You're burning considerably more calories walking on grass or in the woods than on paved surfaces, since the demands on your strength and coordination are greater.

20th Day

Biceps, Triceps – getting your arms into top shape

Let's move

Choose one of the cardio-moves (shown starting on page 18) to get warmed up in less than 60 seconds.

Let's work

1 REVERSE CURLS

→ You're standing upright with one foot slightly in front of the other, your knees slightly bent, and

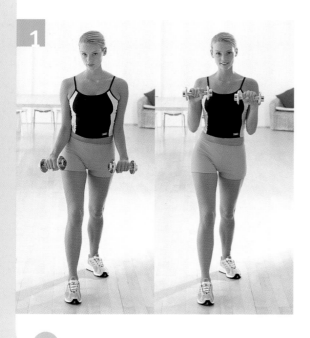

your chest raised. Tense your stomach muscles and pull your shoulders backwards and downwards. Lower your chin a bit and keep your eyes focussed forward.

→ Keep both arms hanging down slightly bent, with the elbows close to your upper body.

→ Now bring the weights up to your shoulders. When doing this make sure that your hands remain constantly in a straight line with your lower arm. Do not bend your wrists.

→ Then slowly return to starting position without extending your arms totally; this maintains the tension in the biceps, thus improving the training result.

→ Do two to three sets of 10 to 15 reps.

Careful: For this exercise, grasp the dumbbells with the backs of your hands facing forwards. Through this type of grip you're working not only the lower arms, but also two other muscles which support the biceps in bending the arm.

2 SYNCHRONIZED KICK BACKS

→ From standing position bend your upper body forward until it's almost parallel to the floor. Pull your stomach in and up towards your sternum. You're holding a weight in each hand.

→ Now bend your arms so that the upper arms are parallel to your body and the lower arms are pointing towards the floor.

→ In addition, stand on the tips of your toes and extend yourself as far as possible. Stretch your arms and your entire body upwards.

→ Feel how your body stretches from your upper arms, through your shoulders – right down to your calves.

→ Hold this position for 10 to 15 seconds and repeat once or twice.

→ Then move both arms backwards until they're totally extended and your shoulders, elbows, and wrists form a straight line. During the first rep of this exercise you'll immediately feel how the triceps are being worked on, even if you use very light weights.

→ Do two to three sets of 10 to 15 reps.

Advanced: Hold the tension for one or two seconds before slowly bringing the weights back down.

→ To two to three sets of 10 to 15 reps.

Let's stretch

3 BODY STRETCH

→ Standing fully erect, raise your chest forcefully as far as you can. Your shoulders are relaxed.

→ Now raise both arms and stretch them overhead. Intertwine your fingers so that the palms of your hands are facing up.

TIP **It's best to do those exercises** which at the beginning are more difficult for you in front of a mirror. That way you can better check your movements.

93

Inline Skating:
get roaring!

So jogging isn't fast enough for you? Then what about skating? This fast activity on eight thin wheels is an ideal workout for your heart and circulation, and it's also easy on the joints. The smooth sequence of movements trains your strength, stamina, coordination and sense of balance, while at the same time working on flabby deposits. You'll be able to notice how the muscles and tissues particularly around the buttocks and legs are quickly toned.

Positive results, however, depend on mastery of basic techniques. It's a chilling fact that about one fourth of all beginners aren't able to brake properly, and, to make matters worse, they don't even wear protective gear. It's no wonder then that dangerous falls are common among beginners. So remember, safety first. Start out by practicing in schoolyards or unused parking lots until you've developed a safe braking technique.

Don't underestimate the danger of injuring yourself: head protection, knee, elbow and wrist pads are absolutely essential. Even if you feel secure, you should be skating only fast enough to be able to stop easily when called at any moment. Always keep within the range of your abilities; you're not protected in a collision, so it's up to you to be alert and to skate defensively.

IT'S ALL IN THE TECHNIQUE

When skating don't let your legs do all the work. By moving your arms loosely in synch, and skillfully shifting the position of your upper body – not just for balance, but also to get more power – you can use inline skating as a tool for shaping your body. To trim down stomach and buttocks to your ideal, pay attention to the angle

On the road with eight wheels. It's fun, it keeps you fit, and it's more and more popular. Go ahead and try inline skating for yourself.

TIP

How to calculate your ideal personal training pulse (see page 83) for inline skating: resting pulse + (220 − 3/4 your age − resting pulse) · 0.6

at which you're bending your hips, knees, and ankles.

The position of the knee, for example, is important in training the leg and buttock muscles, while the angle of the hip determines how the back muscles and abdominals are used. As a rule of thumb, the smaller the angle, the greater the stress on the muscle – and the greater the amount of calories being burned.

IMPORTANT:
HOW TO COME TO A STOP

You can come to a safe stop using the following maneuvers: the heel stop is the simplest and most effective technique for a beginner. To do it, first shift your weight onto the skate which doesn't have a brake pad. Then roll the braking skate forward, tilt it back past the last wheel (extending your leg) and put your weight onto it. The more pressure you put on the brake, the quicker you'll stop moving.

A good alternative when you're moving at moderate speed is the snowplow stop. It works on the same principle as the so-called snowplow used by skiers. Both legs are extended and spread apart. At the same time you put pressure on your heels. Increase the pressure as your skates begin to move inwards with their tips towards each other.

A basic rule in unexpected situations is: change direction before braking. Try always to veer to the right – that is, away from traffic. If you can't stop at all, then it's better to fall onto the railing than risk an uncontrolled crash. ■

Eight wheels – get them rolling!

Safe, sporty, fast: these six tips are a sure way to have fun!

➜ **Don't buy skates from a chain store.** Only a sports shop can give you competent advice and quality. Never buy skates without rubber brakes, because they're the only ones that are suitable for all novices.

➜ **During your obligatory test run** wear only thin socks. If your socks are too thick your feet won't get a firm hold inside the skates. It's most important that the skates hold your heels safely and firmly. In no case should they rub against the heel – that would cause blisters. A free space of 0.5 inches around the toes is OK.

➜ **After the boot has been laced** up the feet must not slide back and forth. Also make sure that there's enough support around the ankles.

➜ **To get to your feet easily** after putting on your skates: from a kneeling position bring up one bent leg. Using the opposite hand on the ground to support yourself, raise yourself slowly.

➜ **Check your starting position:** The skates are apart at shoulder width – make sure that your feet aren't tilted in or out. Then shift your weight slightly forward. You should now notice your shins pressing against the tongue of the shoe. Your weight is distributed evenly between toes and heels. Check your position by looking down past your kneecaps. Can you just make out the tips of your feet? Great, then you're ready to get rolling.

➜ **If you really want to get moving** on your wheels you should bend your upper body slightly forward and keep the skates pointed parallel in the direction you're going. You obtain the necessary momentum by using your heels to push firmly out to the sides. Here's a tip: the smoother you make the transition from gliding easily to pushing forcefully, the more efficient your skating pace becomes.

21st Day

Nice legs – tight buttocks

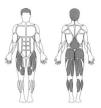

Let's move

Choose one of the cardio-moves (shown starting on page 18) to get warmed up in less than 60 seconds.

Let's work

1 ONE-LEGGED KNEE BENDS

→ Stand in front of a chair at about a step's distance. Bend one knee backwards and rest the top of the foot on the seat. After you've stabilized your

position raise your chest and concentrate on keeping your back upright.

→ Now bend the knee of the front leg far enough for the thigh to become parallel to the floor. Hold briefly at the lowest point, then slowly raise yourself. Careful: your knee joint should not project beyond your toes.

→ Do two to three sets of 15 reps on each side.

Advanced: Make it more difficult by holding your arms stretched out sideways with a weight in each hand. Another possibility of intensifying the exercise is to keep one leg extended in front of you, instead of putting it on a chair.

→ Do two to three sets of 10 to 15 reps per side.

For your information: This demanding exercise is very good for building well-toned muscle. It also improves your coordination and will even out any strength difference between the legs.

TIP **The buttocks are relatively relaxed** when you walk on a flat surface and can be effectively exercised only through upward movement. For most people this means that without additional training the rear tends to sag after the age of 35. Just as with the abdominals, the glutes also need training to keep them looking good.

2 LATERAL LEG LIFTS FOR A TRIM SILHOUETTE

→ Lie down on your left side and rest your head on your lower arm. Place the palm of the right hand in front of you to support your body. Bend the lower lying leg slightly and lift the free leg slightly.

→ Now bring your right leg up as high as you can, keeping your foot bent inward, the toes pointing down slightly.

→ Slowly raise and lower your leg. Then switch sides.

→ Do two to three sets of 15 to 20 reps on each side.

Careful: When lifting the leg don't let the hips tilt forward or backward.

Advanced: Special ankle weights (available in sports shops) give additional resistance.

Let's stretch

3 LYING GLUTES STRETCH

→ Lie down comfortably on your back, extend your right leg upwards, and place your bent left leg over your right thigh.

→ Now grasp your right thigh in both hands and pull the leg carefully towards you. At the same time press the knee of the bent left leg in the opposite direction, away from the body.

→ Gradually release the tension. Then switch leg position and repeat the entire sequence of movements on the other side.

TIP **By keeping your hands on your hips** while doing leg lifts you're able to concentrate wholly on the leg work and you're improving your coordination.

→ Hold the stretch for 10 to 15 seconds on each side and repeat once or twice.

"Always bear in mind that your own
resolution to success is more important
than any other one thing"
(President Abraham Lincoln)

4th Week

Despite good intentions we're sometimes weak, and when that happens we're usually ready with an excuse. It's other people's fault that we occasionally have problems finding even eight minutes in our schedule for a workout. Stop right now! What's the point in looking for a scapegoat? It only makes it harder to see or feel any progress, and then your motivation is gone. You should look for solutions instead. Try getting up 15 minutes earlier to give yourself more time, or have a talk with your boss to clear things up if he's always demanding overtime from you.

When you make your plans include the possibility of setbacks and momentary weakness. Nobody's perfect. A bad day or a sore muscle is no reason to give up totally. Stick to your regular workouts, because then they become something as natural as eating or brushing your teeth. That way you've defeated the inner slob and you've turned a healthy lifestyle into a habit.

22nd Day

Quick workout for chest & back

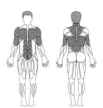

Let's move

Choose one of the cardio-moves (shown starting on page 18) to get warmed up in less than 60 seconds.

Let's work

1 BASIC PUSHUPS

→ Starting position is lying face down. Place your hands palms down on the floor approximately beneath your shoulders. Now tense your arms, thus raising your body from the floor. Distribute your weight evenly between toes and hands. Your fingers are pointing forward the whole time. Head, neck, spine, buttocks and knees all form a straight line, and your stomach muscles are tensed.

→ When doing pushups the head should always form a straight line with the body. You're looking down in order to avoid neck cramps. You should also make sure that your buttocks aren't hanging down or protruding upwards.

→ Now lower your upper body slowly until the tip of your nose almost touches the floor. In order to get the most out of the chest muscles, you should carry out this exercise with the greatest possible range of movement. The further you lower yourself, the more intensive the workout!

→ Then push yourself up again, but without fully extending your arms. At the highest point, you keep your elbows slightly bent, so that the tension in your chest, shoulders and triceps is maintained.

→ Do two to three sets of 10 to 15 pushups.

Advanced: At first start out from the starting position for basic pushups. To increase the difficulty, now put one foot on the heel of the other foot, so that your body weight is now resting on only three points.

→ Do two to three sets of 10 to 15 reps.

ONE-ARMED ROWING

→ Take a long step forward with your left leg. Put your left hand on the leg to support yourself. The arm is slightly bent. Your back is straight, your stomach tensed.

→ In your right hand you're holding a dumbbell, with your hand facing inward.

→ While exhaling, pull the weight up towards your body until the hand is at the level of your lower ribs. While doing this, keep your elbows close to your body and don't let your shoulders sag from the weight.

→ Intensively work on one side first, then switch hands and standing positions.

→ Do two to three sets of 10 to 15 reps.

Let's stretch

YOGA STRETCH

→ From a standing position bring the palms of your hand together behind your back. Your fingers are pointing downwards.

→ Now very gently move your elbows back as far as you can. Your back remains upright all this time. Exert your chest upwards.

→ Hold the extension for ten seconds and repeat once or twice.

Vitamins –
an invisible pick-me-up

For many people vitamins are the ultimate symbol of healthy food. And in fact our bodies cannot function without these invisible, neutral-tasting, feather-light substances. They participate in every metabolic process. They don't supply any energy in themselves, but they ensure that everything runs smoothly – and you need only tiny amounts of them. They're important for, among other things, the composition of blood, your eyesight, healthy skin and hair, and the formation of body tissues. In total there are 13 vitamins, none of which are produced by the body itself, which means you have to obtain them from your daily diet.

There are basically two types of vitamins: water-soluble and fat-soluble. Water-soluble vitamins can be stored by the body for only a short period of time. Vitamin C belongs to this group, as does the so-called vitamin B complex, which includes vitamins B1, B2, B6, and B12, as well as niacin, pantothenic acid, folic acid, and biotin.

The fat-soluble group includes vitamins A, D, E and K. The body is able to absorb these only when they are connected to fat. But even the smallest amounts of fat are enough to ensure that they reach the body's cells. For example, the amount of fat in a cup of yogurt eaten two hours before or after you've had a carrot is quite sufficient for absorption. Likewise, the olive oil in salad dressing is enough for the vitamins in lettuce.

You shouldn't ingest excess quantities of fat-soluble vitamins, because, unlike water-soluble vitamins, in higher doses they can't be excreted by the body. Instead, they're deposited in fatty tissues and the liver. There is then an oversupply of them. So, too much doesn't help much.

Snacks that do you good: fresh snacks are sweet and healthy and give you enjoyment that you won't regret later.

TIP **Is it actually possible to buy** fresh fruit and vegetables every day? If not, then the right alternative to fresh is frozen. For example, up to 80 percent of vitamin C content is preserved by deep freezing. Vitamins on the rocks! It's better than lettuce or spinach that's been sitting around for two or three days.

HOW MANY VITAMINS SHOULD I BE GETTING?

Basically, each person has his own individual requirement of vitamins and minerals (see also starting page 106). This depends on a person's height, weight and general health, but also on his lifestyle. The best supply of vitamins always comes from fruits and vegetables. You can also get more or less high doses of these essential nutrients in meat, fish, grains and dairy products. Examples of good sources of the B vitamins are whole grain products, cereals, and fish.

The bottom line: Instead of taking vitamin pills, nourish yourself with the widest variety of foods nature has to offer. Look for foods which are in season. It's precisely the interplay of countless substances that makes our food so valuable.

Vitamins A, C and E play a particularly special role. They can protect us against attack from so-called free radicals. It doesn't matter whether it's the aging process, illnesses such as cancer, heart disease or other ailments – these aggressive oxygen compounds are always involved. They attack cell structures, protein molecules, and even the genetic makeup. The greater the individual load from everyday stress, pollution or an unhealthy lifestyle, the greater the damage that free radicals can cause.

Fortunately you can protect yourself from them. Vitamins C, E, as well as A, in the form of beta-carotene, are called anti-oxidants, and they are your "fighters" against free radicals. ■

Fitness from the kitchen

Vitamins are sensitive – it's not unusual for food to lose over 50 percent of its vitamins through improper storage or preparation. That's why you should observe the following buying, cooking and storage tips to help keep vitamins intact.

➜ **Keep it natural.** Eat food in it's most natural state. The more processing food has gone through, the fewer vitamins are left in it.

➜ **Go with the times.** You should opt for fresh market produce from your area, according to the season. Exotic fruits and vegetables are often treated with pesticides, since they have to be transported great distances.

➜ **Go shopping at the last minute.** It's better to go shopping for food as frequently as possible than to store food for a longer period of time. When you're buying to stock up, store vitamin-rich foods in a cool, dark space. The only exceptions are tropical fruits such as oranges and bananas.

➜ **Don't scrub!** Remove only what you have to from fruits and vegetables. Most of the vitamins are under the skin. And please don't wash too thoroughly. That will simply rinse away any water-soluble vitamins.

➜ **Get moving in the kitchen!** Don't start dicing until shortly before you eat. By cutting up vegetables and lettuce you're enlarging their surfaces. If you rinse them after cutting, then you're washing away a great deal of vitamins from the cut surfaces.

➜ **Use gentle cooking methods.** Cooking using aluminum foil, Dutch ovens, stainless steel cookware, pressure cookers and steamers preserves vitamins.

➜ **Play it safe.** To get the total organic effect, when preparing food always reuse the water in which it has been boiled.

103

23rd Day

Attractive shoulders and a trim waistline

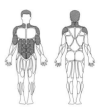

Let's move

Choose one of the cardio-moves (shown starting on page 18) to get warmed up in less than 60 seconds.

Let's work

1 UPRIGHT ROWING

→ You're standing up straight, your feet are apart at shoulder width, and your knees are slightly bent.

Your arms are slightly bent and you're holding a dumbbell at hip level in each hand. Your palms are facing in towards your body.

→ Now bring the weights in a rowing motion close along your body up to the height of your collarbone. During this movement your elbows are pointing upwards.

→ Gently tilt your upper body a bit forward. Your back should however remain straight. Then return your arms to the starting position.

→ Do two to three sets of 10 to 15 reps.

Careful: Exhale each time you lift the weights and continue with your natural breathing rhythm.

2 REVERSE CURLS

→ Lie down on your back and stretch your legs straight out towards the ceiling. To help you keep your balance, spread your arms out to the sides and rest them on the floor. Now lift the buttocks slowly – without swinging! – from the floor.

→ When making this movement try to crumple your abdomen like an accordion, while at the same time moving your knees towards your chest. What's important in this exercise is not the range of movement, but its correct performance.

→ Through the contraction of the stomach muscles the lower back is curled up some-what.

→ Do two to three sets of eight to ten reps.

TIP **Concentrated breathing** is the secret formula for relaxation and extra power (see also breathing exercises on page 79). If you breathe carefully during every exercise you'll soon notice how a feeling of relaxation takes over, how your strength building workouts become more effective, and how the stretching exercises have a noticeable effect.

TIP **Concentrate** and feel your abdominal muscles working. Put your hand on your muscles; this will help you to perceive more intensely the tension in your stomach muscles and to check the exercise movements. It helps you become more aware of your body and, according to the latest findings, it increases the effectiveness of your workouts.

For your information: In this exercise a movement of only a few inches is enough to train your abdominals effectively.

Let's stretch

3 SHOULDER PULL

→ Stand up in a steady position with your knees slightly bent. Now fold your arms behind your buttocks or use one hand to grasp the opposite wrist.

→ Now forcefully pull both arms backwards and downwards as far as you can. Supplement this movement further by pushing your shoulders downwards.

→ During this extension, your back remains very straight and your chest is raised. Continue breathing deeply and evenly.

→ Hold the extension for 10 to 15 seconds and repeat once or twice.

Minerals –
Power in a small package

Tired, unconcentrated, depressed – without minerals we'd soon be totally beat. Even though they make up only about nine pounds of our bodyweight, that's nine pounds which we absolutely don't want to lose! Minerals are inorganic elements that are as small and just as essential to life as vitamins are (see from page 102). There are over 20 types, and each one plays a specific role in our bodies. Minerals themselves don't supply any nutritional energy, but without these substances we wouldn't even be able to bat an eyelid. Whether it's digestion, reproduction or the intellect, minerals are always involved. They are important components of our muscles and nerves, bones and teeth, and they help in blood formation and in transporting oxygen in the blood. Since your body is not able to create minerals on its own, and actually loses them with each drop of bodily fluids, it's up to you to obtain the necessary quantities in your daily food.

IT'S THE RIGHT COMBINATION THAT COUNTS

Minerals are divided into two types: macro-elements and trace elements. The difference lies in the quantity of the particular mineral found in our bodies. We need relatively large quantities of "minerals" or macro-elements (such as calcium and magnesium), while we need only a few micrograms of trace elements (such as zinc and chromium). Nevertheless, we're never really sure we're getting the amounts we require. There are several reasons for this: stress, alcohol, and a monotonous diet can all upset our nutritional budget. Even when we use fresh ingredients we often pour minerals down the drain when we wash and boil food. That's why it's not necessary to check nutrition charts constantly for the right portions. In order to ensure that you're getting the right amount of nutrients, diversity is once again the key. Try to eat as wide a variety of fresh, unprocessed food as you can.

Here's what a daily plan offering plenty of minerals might look like: five handful-sized servings of fruit and vegetables, low fat dairy products (such

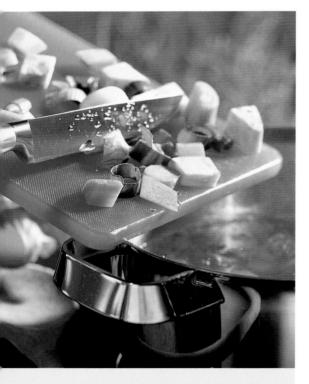

Chopped smoothly, served quickly: fix food the right way, and it will keep its power.

TIP

If you believed the ads, you'd think that a single mineral tablet would be enough to give you energy for the whole day. But it's not quite that simple: very often pill formulas aren't based on solid scientific evidence and they are no substitute for a balanced diet.

as, for example, two glasses of milk, 2 slices of cheese), at least six servings of whole-grain products (for example three slices of bread, one serving of whole-grain cereal, 30 grams of rice), as well as fish and meat twice a week.

Another tip: You should always reach for fresh food instead of a pill (see also box above).

AN OVERVIEW OF FIVE IMPORTANT HELPERS

→ Magnesium activates over 300 enzymes, helps in metabolizing energy, in the interaction of nerves and muscles, and it protects against heart disease. It's found abundantly in whole-grain products, legumes, green vegetables, milk, fish, bananas and berries. Magnesium-rich mineral water is also useful.

→ Calcium as a building material strengthens our bones and also influences muscles, nerves and blood clotting. A lack of it causes the body to obtain calcium from the bones, which thus become brittle. Further symptoms of lack of calcium: you become nervous and weak, and you suffer from circulatory problems. Large amounts of calcium are found in milk and dairy products, and also in sesame seeds, berries, whole grains, dried fruit, and vegetables, especially broccoli, leeks, and spinach.

→ Iron gives us stamina. It is essential for the transport of oxygen in the blood and is important for the entire immune system. Lack of it may cause loss of appetite, tiredness, and anemia. Since iron from vegetable sources is best absorbed by the body in combination with vitamin C, you should always include that in your meals: for example, lemon juice in a fresh salad, or a glass of orange juice or a fruit salad after your main meal.

→ Iodine keeps cells running smoothly. This mineral associated with the thyroid gland is vital for cells and for regulating the metabolism, as well as for the heart, lungs, kidneys and muscles. Too little makes you tired and nervous, and your performance and concentration suffer. Good iodine suppliers are seafood, seaweed, meat and dairy products.

→ Zinc helps wounds heal faster. Too little may result in slow healing of injuries and a weakened immune system. Over 300 enzymes depend on a supply of zinc. During periods of psychological and physical stress, increased amounts of zinc are excreted in urine. Make sure to get enough of it in whole grains, fish and shellfish. ▪

Don't miss out on anything

Eight tricks to help you coax more nutrients from food:

→ **Wash lettuce and vegetables** before they're chopped. Otherwise you'll be rinsing most of their minerals away.

→ **When peeling oranges don't remove the white tissue** under the peel; this is where minerals and vitamins are concentrated.

→ **It's better to grill, steam, blanch or stew,** than to boil. It preserves more minerals.

→ **Fish is best when steamed in aluminum foil** – and don't combine it with cabbage. This maintains its iodine content and your body will absorb it better.

→ **Fresh and frozen foods** contain considerably more minerals than canned.

→ **Use sharp knives.** They damage fewer cells and thus keep losses at a minimum.

→ **Save the liquids** that result from cooking to make soups or sauces later.

→ **Don't eat convenience foods often,** since the more foods are processed the more they lose their minerals.

24th Day

Biceps, Triceps – getting your arms into top shape

Let's move

Choose one of the cardio-moves (shown starting on page 18) to get warmed up in less than 60 seconds.

Let's work

1 ROTATING CURLS

→ From a standing position, put one foot slightly forward. Your arms are only slightly bent and are close to your body. You're holding a dumbbell in each hand. In starting position, your hands are facing inwards.

→ Flex your biceps and first bring one arm with the weight slowly up to shoulder level.

→ At about thigh level begin each time to rotate your lower arm, so that in the end position the inside of the hand is facing the shoulder. The advantage of this: the rotation of the lower arm and the bending of the elbow are doubly hard on the biceps, which means that your arms are being particularly well worked on.

→ Now bring the dumbbell slowly back to opening position without completely extending your arm. In doing this you rotate your hand back to starting position (hands facing inwards towards the body). At the same time bend the other arm up to the shoulder.

→ Continue alternating moving your arms in a flowing movement to the shoulder.

→ Do two to three sets of 10 to 15 reps on each side.

TIP **With this exercise** you have the possibility of observing closely the movement of each side of the body. Focus on keeping the arms from swinging next to the body. Shoulders and upper arms should be kept still.

→ Now stretch your arms back upwards, without stretching the elbows out. Don't spread out the upper arms – they stay close to your head.

→ Alternate bending and stretching the arms slowly in a fluid sequence.

→ Do two to three sets of 10 to 15 reps.

Let's stretch

3 BENT-OVER CHEST AND ARMS STRETCH

→ At first, crouch down in front of the mat, and then bend your upper body forward and stretch out your arms in front of you. Your hands lie on their sides with the thumbs on top.

→ After your arms are totally extended and a 90 degree angle has formed between the upper and lower leg, pull your shoulders back and lower your chest further towards the floor. During this your buttocks remain directly above your knees.

→ Hold the extension for ten to fifteen seconds and repeat once or twice.

2 TRICEPS CURLS

→ Sit on a chair with your back straight, your stomach muscles tensed, and your chest raised. Your feet are flat on the floor and apart at hip width.

→ With both arms slightly bent and your hands bent back, bring a dumbbell up and behind your head. Your thumbs are gripping the shaft, and one end of the dumbbell is resting on your palms. The other end is hanging down (see photo above).

→ Now bend both elbows to bring the dumbbell down until it's behind your neck. While doing this keep your upper arms as close as you can to your head.

TIP **By resting your arms** on a chair or – from a standing position – on a window sill or other raised platform, you can intensify this exercise.

From morning till night:
keep fit throughout the day

What, when, and how you eat can be decisive in making progress. If you want to feel healthy, strive to find the perfect balance of fat, carbohydrates, protein, vitamins and minerals. Here are a few more tips for perfect timing in food matters.

A HEALTHY START

Good morning. Energy reserves which were used up during sleep are restocked for the day with a well-balanced breakfast. This is important because in the next hours you'll need your concentration and power. Hearty rolled oats with yogurt or other low-fat dairy products make for a fit start to the day. A spoonful of bran added to whole-grain cereal will give you the right dose of folic acid to help you metabolize protein.

On the other hand, processed corn flakes and cereals, rolls or a baguette with jam: these are typical breakfast items that you should avoid. That's because it's especially in the morning that sugar and starches trigger a large release of insulin. You start to crave sugary foods – and you've just set yourself up for a day of pigging out.

As a rule, whole-wheat bread should be your first choice. And you should never leave home without having had breakfast first. Without its morning "input" your body soon panics and then switches right away to low gear. With an unpleasant effect: your body doesn't really start burning fat.

MID-MORNING SNACKS

Hardly anybody can work at full strength right through to lunchtime. It's actually normal for your abilities to sag a bit (see also page 22). So go ahead and give yourself a short break and enjoy a little between-meal snack. How about one of the following?

→ Cottage cheese with apple or banana slices will give you longer lasting energy than a chocolate bar or cookies.

No matter what you're having, even a small snack, try to arrange it attractively. It'll wake up your appetite for healthy food.

> **Breakfast cereal** made from whole grains which have soaked overnight is especially healthy and filling. Yogurt and fresh fruit will always give it variety.

→ Yogurt with a tablespoonful of whole-grain cereal supplies valuable protein.

→ Dried dates or apricots are a real secret weapon against the morning slump. Even small amounts are effective for a quick energy boost and better concentration.

→ Reach for fresh vegetables: instead of cold cuts or cheese put cucumber or tomato on your bread.

→ Why don't you try vegetable sticks with a herb yogurt dip?

→ A tip for all you chocolate fans: bittersweet chocolate with a high proportion of cocoa (at least 70 percent) has a considerably lower glycemic index (see page 59) than milk chocolate.

LUNCHTIME – THE POWER BOOST

Stewing, grilling, baking without added fat, steaming in aluminum foil or frying in non-stick pans – all ways to cut down on fat and not on flavor! Also, vegetable oils should be your first choice for cooking. And of course you can eat all the vegetables you want, since the high fiber content in veggies helps your body to slim down naturally.

An even easier solution is a whole-wheat sandwich filled with salmon slices, turkey breast or low-fat cheese – pepped up with cucumbers and lettuce. The combination of grains, low-fat protein and fresh vegetables is guaranteed to supply you with the power you need for the second half of the day. Also good: a mixed salad with yogurt dressing and a whole-grain roll. And be consistent when it comes to dessert: whenever possible, go for fresh fruit.

DINNERTIME: A GOOD FINISH

If lunch was the main meal of the day, then dinner should be light. Do you like it cool and crisp? A salad of raw vegetables together with bread and cheese is just the thing. If you'd like something warm, then serve yourself plenty of vegetables along with some meat or fish.

A tip for all you pasta fans: instead of boiling spaghetti until it's soft, have it al dente. This way the body absorbs the carbohydrates more slowly and you won't get hungry again so soon. ■

Slimming strategies for lunch

Lunchtime for many people means a quick bite – or the cafeteria. Here's how to avoid some of the dangers awaiting you there:

→ **Keep away from casseroles** – there's often a good reason why only the cook knows what's in them, and they usually contain too much fat.

→ **Small portions of meat and gravy** are enough. Three quarters of your plate should be taken up by vegetables, whole-wheat pasta, or brown rice.

→ **Fries, hash browns, and potato pancakes** slow down your performance, so you should leave them alone.

→ **If you want to play it safe with your health** treat yourself regularly to a large salad for lunch. Instead of fatty dressing, vinegar and a little oil will do just fine.

→ **For dessert opt for fruit** over cake – and vitamins over sugar.

25th Day

Nice legs – tight buttocks

Let's move

Choose one of the cardio-moves (shown starting on page 18) to get warmed up in less than 60 seconds.

Let's work

1 STEP-UPS

→ You start in standing position. If you can handle it, hold a weight in each hand at your sides. Otherwise, use your arms for balance.

Place a foot onto the center of a stable stool or a chair.
→ Keep your body upright and your stomach tensed while you press down forcefully on the heel of the raised foot, bringing both legs onto the chair. Your rear leg should help you in maintaining balance.
→ Then reverse the movement by slowly and carefully returning the first leg to the starting position.
→ Let the rear foot touch the floor only briefly before you repeat the movement. The energy for this comes exclusively from the leg and buttock muscles, and you're using your upper body only to keep your balance.
→ Repeat the sequence with the other foot.
→ Do two to three sets of 15 to 20 reps on each side.

Advanced: Continue using the strength of your standing leg to raise yourself onto the chair. Only this time thrust the knee up above hip level when climbing. Hold briefly, then descend using the same leg. Change sides after each set.
→ Do two to three sets of 10 to 15 reps on each side.

2 BENT LEG HIP RAISE

→ Starting position is on all fours – this works on the muscles of the entire torso. Your head is straight, and your stomach is tensed tightly enough for your back not to curve in. Now shift

your weight a little to the right, so that you're able to lift your left leg from the floor.

→ Now lift your left leg to the side without moving your hips along with it. Your back remains very straight. Careful: don't let your lower back curve in.

→ Slowly lower the leg and switch sides after each set.

→ Do two to three sets of 15 to 20 reps per side.

Advanced: Lift the leg stretched out instead of bent to the side, and raise it until it's parallel to the floor.

→ You can also make this exercise harder by using ankle weights.

→ Do two to three sets of 10 to 15 reps on each side.

Let's stretch

3 HIP FLEXOR EXTENSION

→ Bring your right foot forward in a long step. While doing this lower your left knee and the back of the left foot onto the mat. Rest both hands on your right thigh to support yourself and keep your upper body upright.

→ Then shift into an extended position by moving your hips forward and downward a bit every time you exhale. In addition, you can slide your left thigh further back.

→ Repeat the exercise with the other side of the body.

→ Hold the extension for 10 to 15 seconds and repeat twice on each side.

TIP

To vary the exercise you can rest the front leg on a chair.

Buy healthy:
Low calorie shopping

You've called it a day! It's time to breathe easy, go home and pamper yourself. Then in your mind you quickly go through the contents of your kitchen fridge – no way! A glance at your watch and you're thrown into a panic. There's only half an hour left for shopping if you don't want to eat takeaway.

You have to be fast. And don't forget, you did say you were going to start a healthier, well-balanced diet. But don't panic – with a few tricks in the supermarket you can already start outwitting the calories. After all, at some point in time you are going to eat everything you put into the shopping cart.

So as long as you avoid slipping up in the supermarket and choose the right items from the wide selection available, you'll be able to avoid making a big mistake later at the fridge.

DEFEND YOURSELF AGAINST CALORIES – FIRST, SOME TRICKS

First tip: always take along a shopping list! Do you think it's dumb to run around with a piece of paper? Well, it will save you time and nerves. When you've put down on a list all your necessary food items, you won't succumb to the lures of impulse buying. With your shopping list in hand you can kiss temptation goodbye.

Tip number two: Leave your hunger at home. Do you suddenly notice your favorite chocolate bar waiting for you at the checkout? An empty stomach will give you bad advice in the supermarket! Your brain is defenseless against a growling belly. Driven by hunger, it's easy for you to grab junk food that you really don't need. So before you go shopping, make sure you have a snack: for example, some fruit. ■

Leave the supermarket a winner – you've resisted unhealthy temptation!

The agony of choice – finding your way through the supermarket

A brief guide with a few healthy tips to help you find your way through the shopping jungle.

→ **Go whole-grain,** especially when it comes to spaghetti, penne and tagliatelle. Whole-wheat pasta is particularly rich in valuable protein and minerals, and it has double the fiber of regular pasta. But if you really don't like brown noodles, then go for real Italian pasta. The high-quality long chained carbohydrates (see from page 58) in the ingredients of traditional pasta – flour from durum wheat, salt and water – keep you feeling full for a long time.

→ **A lean mix.** Buy lean meats, such as cold cuts from poultry, turkey breast, and ham, raw or cooked, without fat around the edges. You should avoid meat products such as liverwurst or sausages that have gone through the meat grinder. The rule here is, the finer the texture, the fatter the meat. Also choose leaner varieties of cheese and dairy products. Products with less than 30 percent fat solids are the ones to put into your shopping cart.

→ **Have your cold cuts sliced thin** – that way you keep from fattening up at the deli counter. If you don't happen to have an electric slicer in your kitchen, make sure your deli meats and cheeses are cut thin at the counter. People who slice at home tend to be generous with the slices, and that's just fat that will make its way to your hips.

→ **Snacking packs on pounds.** Don't buy anything you won't eat in the next few days. When you stockpile chips and chocolate, sooner or later you're going to polish them off. But if your larder is empty, at least you'll have to get off the couch to go to the nearest convenience store. And who knows? Maybe on the way you'll remember the promises you made.

→ **Read the small print.** If animal fats are the first item on the list of ingredients, you can be sure the product is loaded with saturated fat. It's better not to touch it. Careful: convenience foods such as frozen pizza or chocolate pudding are particularly rich in hidden fat. Here it's really worth taking the trouble to read the fine print.

→ **Careful with "lite" products!** "Lite" can have many meanings: lightly whipped, easy to digest, less sugar, or sometimes even less fat. The word has no legal definition and can mean anything. Diet margarine, for example, is often as fatty (80 percent fat) as regular. But there are alternatives: sour cream (30 percent), low-fat cream cheese (15 percent), cottage cheese (5 percent) or even curd cheese (as low as 0.3 percent fat solids) are all good spreads.

→ **Whole foods.** As a rule, the more thoroughly a food has been processed, the fewer nutrients it contains. That doesn't mean you have to make your own cereal out of whole grains, but you should always look out for high-quality, whole foods. It's already a good start when you put whole-wheat instead of white bread into your shopping cart. Or use pure fruit juice, with or without water, to quench your thirst, instead of a soft drink.

→ **Choose the icy alternative.** Avoid convenience foods from cans. Use frozen foods instead. Often they contain even more vitamins than fresh fruit from the produce department, because they're deep frozen right after harvesting.

→ **Help for people with a sweet tooth.** For you, the moment of truth arrives at the candy section. Can you remain steady? If not, then at least try out untreated, dried fruit. It's sweet and tasty. At about 255 calories per 100 grams it may not be exactly low calorie, but it's by far the healthiest sweet snack.

26th Day

Quick workout for chest & back

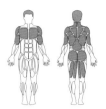

Let's move

Choose one of the cardio-moves (shown starting on page 18) to get warmed up in less than 60 seconds.

Let's work

1 CHEST PUSHUPS

→ Begin the exercise by doing standing butterflys, which you already learned on day 2 (see page 20): you're standing upright, with your legs apart at shoulder width. In each hand you're holding a dumbbell. Now lift the weights out from your body on either side until you reach shoulder level. From this position bend your lower arm upwards until it is vertical.

→ Bring your tensed arms together in front of your body in a semi-circular motion. While doing this, your upper arms must remain at shoulder level and your lower arms bent.

→ Now concentrate on lifting your lower arms up over shoulder level.

→ Flex your pectorals and press your arms tightly against each other. Only then do you bring your arms back down.

→ Do two to three sets of 10 to 15 reps.

2 LIGHT KNEE BENDS WITH LATERAL ROWING

→ Your legs are apart at hip width and you're holding a dumbbell in each hand at about hip level in front of your body.

→ Bend your knees until the thighs are almost horizontal (an 80 degree angle is perfect).

→ Push your buttocks backwards as though you were about to sit down. While doing this, tilt your upper body slightly forward with your chest pushed out. Your stomach is tensed.

→ At the same time, move your elbows backwards and upwards and pull your shoulder blades together. At end position your upper and lower arms are bent at 90 degrees, and your elbows are behind your body.

→ Now extend your legs until they're straight, and bring your arms back in front of your body.

→ Do two to three sets of 10 to 15 reps.

Let's stretch

3 CHEST TWIST

→ You're standing next to a doorframe or a wall, with your feet apart at shoulder width, slightly bent, and one foot slightly forward.

→ Stretch one arm at chest level out to the side so that the hand rests on the wall. Twist your upper body in the opposite direction until you feel a light pull on your chest.

→ Then repeat on the other side.

→ Hold the stretch for 10 to 15 seconds on each side and repeat once or twice.

TIP **In order to stretch** different parts of the chest muscles, change the angle of your arm by resting it lower or higher on the wall.

So long!
Say goodbye to those pounds.

So you want to slim down. No problem. Here are seven tips on how to make every day lighter and more enjoyable.

1 Let's drink to good eating

By taking in plenty of liquids before a meal you're filling your stomach and reining in your hunger. Sometimes when you feel like a snack, what you really want is something to drink. That's because both hunger and thirst are transmitted by the same nerve receptors. So leave the fridge for now and first get yourself a glass of water. You can also drink when you're not thirsty anymore, since with each gulp of water there's less room for chocolate pudding. Yerba mate tea is a secret weapon against excess pounds; it's bitter elements curb the appetite.

2 Take it easy

Before every meal, lower your pace a notch. It takes the brain about 20 minutes before it gets the message, "That's enough. I'm full" from the stomach. Fast eaters manage to put away more food than they have to while they're actually full. So: chew thoroughly and pause now and then (see also tips on page 46).

3 Never go hungry to a party

Prepare your stomach for the coming temptation with a banana or a slice of whole-wheat bread. This way you have something in your stomach and you won't be tempted so easily by lavish buffets. Besides, it'll give you time to pick out the nicest tidbits, thus sparing you a whole load of unnecessary calories.

4 Less is more!

Treat yourself throughout the day to small healthy snacks, instead of topping off the day with a heavy dinner in the evening. Your body reacts to a big meal by increasing insulin production. This leads to a further increase in appetite. It's smarter to try to keep insulin at a steady level. Here's a good idea for stabilizing insulin: if you're feeling hungry, how about some whole-grain cereal or a small salad with sunflower seeds?

5 Really hot!

When your mouth is burning from your lips to your tonsils, naturally you're going to think twice before every bite. But that's not the only reason why spicy food is thinning. Intense spices subdue feelings of hunger! So get yourself to a Thai or Chinese restaurant for lunch. The dishes are so spicy hot that your hunger pangs will diminish in no time. But a good helping of iodine-rich onions will also help, since they work through the thyroid gland to curb your appetite.

If you'd like some heartier fare, you should try a turkey onion stew seasoned with plenty of cayenne pepper and sambal olek. Incidentally, chilies, hot sauce and the like stimulate your blood circulation and thus also burn up to ten percent additional calories.

6 Not too much salt in the soup

It's better not to have the salt shaker near you on the dinner table. These small white grains don't just help raise your blood pressure, they also stimulate your appetite. So use your imagination a bit. By using dried herbs, lemon juice or vinegar on your food, you're living healthier and broadening your taste horizons.

7 You eat with your eyes, too

And that's just fine, because then you can make things lavish. Simply arrange the meal on a large plate and garnish with plenty of salad, crudités or fruit. Right away, your mind interprets this delicious decoration as a lavish spread. Your eye tells the brain, "That's a lot of food!" And this way, you're getting an extra dose of vitamins at the same time.

27th Day

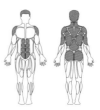

Attractive shoulders and a trim waistline

Let's move

Choose one of the cardio-moves (shown starting on page 18) to get warmed up in less than 60 seconds.

Let's work

1 POWER PRESS FOR STRONG SHOULDERS

→ Use dumbbells with light weights for this exercise, which makes demands on the entire shoulder area.

→ Sit on a chair which has a back, with your torso upright. From this starting position raise your elbows forward up to shoulder level. Your arms are bent upward at a 90 degree angle, with the backs of your hands facing forward.

→ Now press the weights up over your head. At the highest point, your elbows are only minimally bent and the palms of your hands are facing forward – that means you will have rotated your hands 180 degrees forward while lifting the weights.

→ Carefully go back to starting position, rotating your hands back to their original position.

→ Do two to three sets of 10 to 15 reps.

Careful: As with all overhead exercises, you should double check before you start that the weight plates on your dumbbells are securely attached!

Advanced: You can also do this exercise starting from a standing position. Stand with one foot forward to steady yourself.

2 STATIC POWER PUSHUPS

→ Begin by lying face down. Then support yourself with your forearms. The elbows are on the mat, directly below the shoulder joints.

→ Keep your entire body in a straight line from the shoulders to the feet. Your head is facing down

the whole time. Careful: keep your stomach tensed at all times during the exercise to avoid arching your lower back. Nevertheless, be sure to breathe evenly.

→ Do two to three sets of three to four reps.

For your information: This demanding exercise strengthens the stomach and back muscles while at the same time firming your posture.

Advanced: If you can easily do this exercise, then try lifting one leg slightly while your upper body is raised.

→ The exercise gets even harder when you also raise one arm slightly. (The left arm and the right leg at the same time, or vice versa.)

→ Do two to three sets of three to four reps.

Let's stretch

3 COMBINED LEG AND TORSO STRETCH

→ Stand with a chair or stool to your side and place the nearest foot on the seat of the chair. The knee of your standing leg is slightly bent.

→ Now stretch the outer arm high over your head. The other arm is bent with the hand resting on your waist. Now slide the foot on the chair further to the side and bend your upper body in the same direction.

→ Then it's the other leg's turn.

→ Hold the extension on each side for ten seconds and repeat once or twice.

TIP

Remember, stretching is not a competitive sport! The sole purpose of stretching exercises is to help you feel better.

The outlook:
how to continue

Congratulations! You've made it, and you've come a long way towards having the body you've always wanted. Are you feeling better than before? That's great! Keep on the path that you've set for yourself, follow some of our tips now and then to keep up your spirits, and absolutely avoid falling back into your old routine. After all, you must have been pleased to notice some improvements over the past few weeks: there's no trace of muscle aches, and you have no difficulty now in mastering exercises which earlier would have put your coordination to a hard test. In short, you're simply a lot fitter than before.

But the most important thing is that you've proven to yourself that you're able to take responsibility for your body, develop a new and deeper awareness of it, and expand your limits bit by bit. If you want, you can test yourself again using our fitness check (see page 126).

NOW TO THE NEXT ROUND

You've kept going! And your own body has proved a fundamental rule of athletic training, namely, that your body is capable of adapting to an increased workload. It reacts to challenges by quickly increasing the performance you desire.

On the other hand, this also means that you should continue giving your muscles, heart, and circulatory system new and interesting tasks if you wish to maintain, or even increase, your strength. The bottom line: the better you get, the harder you have to train in order to progress. But don't worry; after only four weeks your period of success is far from over. If you continue to build on the level of fitness you've already reached, giving your body the time it needs and treating yourself to the entire four week plan a second

After four weeks you can show yourself off – and you'll have fun continuing with your new hobby.

> **TIP**
> **Try out dynamic stretching:**
> Bring the muscle into a position where
> you can feel it pulling slightly. Then
> from end position release slowly and
> carefully for 10 to 15 seconds. Repeat
> once.

time (with perhaps a few changes), you'll come closer step by step to the ideal body you've worked for. And the great thing about it is that the effort required will remain small compared to the benefits you reap.

TREAT YOURSELF TO MORE!

Don't look at your watch; 10 to 15 minutes are always possible. You can be proud of every extra minute you devote to yourself and your fitness program. Aren't you worth the time? Use the workout to give yourself a timeout from everyday stress and obligations. You should consider this time as a valuable investment in yourself. As an extra benefit you'll notice how your motivation will grow along with your progress.

Maybe you've already gotten hooked on one of the endurance sports we've shown and it's become a firm part of your life. Well then, keep sight of your training goals, look forward to the next four weeks, and above all, keep at it! It's worth it!

In the box on the right you'll find a few more tips for advanced training. Careful: these methods are really very demanding. And it's still a basic rule for everybody to keep on the safe side. The correct performance of every exercise is essential to the success of the workout. It's more important than increasing the difficulty. ■

Now you're really working!

Increase the difficulty in the second round. But continue carrying out the exercises carefully.

→ **Give yourself variety:** together with the exercises, under the heading "Advanced" you'll find more difficult variations that will further train your muscles. The desired result is to reach other muscle fibers and thus bring you further into top form.

→ **Do you want more?** You'll get it – increase the scope of your workouts. Do at least three sets per exercise and increase the number of reps.

→ **Give it all you've got!** During the third set work on every last muscle fiber. You should find it difficult to carry out the exercise. So choose a weight that will leave your muscles really exhausted at the end.

→ **The ultimate training kick!** The following small refinements can help make your workouts more varied and individual.

→ **Nice and slow.** The intensity of each set can be increased without additional weight through moving at a concentrated pace: give yourself four seconds to raise the dumbbell – or your body – and five seconds to lower it. Jolting or jerky movements are, as always, taboo.

→ **Burn baby burn!** If you really want to give your muscles a hefty workout, try the following:

First variation: At the end of the last set do a few so-called partial movements. You do this by limiting yourself to exactly that part of the exercise which you feel is the most demanding. Prolong the period of greatest muscle tension.

Second variation: here the efficiency of the exercise is increased by holding the tension of the exercised muscle at the end of a movement for a short moment (one or two seconds).

28th Day

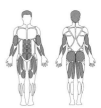

Biceps, Triceps – getting your arms into top shape

Let's move

Choose one of the cardio-moves (shown starting on page 18) to get warmed up in less than 60 seconds.

Let's work

1 POWER DIPS

→ Support yourself by the heels of your hands on the seat of a chair behind your back. Set one foot flat on the floor and stretch out the opposite leg horizontally.

→ To work on your triceps, lower yourself until your upper arms are in a horizontal position. While doing this keep your shoulders lowered.

→ Then stretch your arms out and raise yourself back into starting position. After completing this switch the position of your legs.

→ Do two to three sets of 10 to 15 reps on each side.

2 LUNGES WITH CURLS

→ You're standing upright with your feet apart at about hip width. Your arms are close to your body, and you're holding a dumbbell in each hand. Now take a wide step forward with your left foot.

→ While breathing in deeply through your nose raise your arms up over your sides until the palms of your hands touch. Breathe deeply into your belly and give your lungs enough space to fill up on plenty of oxygen.

→ Now let the air rush audibly back out through your open mouth. While exhaling lower your arms back down and cross them in front of your body.

→ Hold this position for about ten seconds and after a short pause repeat the entire sequence.

→ Now exhale while you bend your legs. At the same time flex your biceps and raise the dumbbells forward up to your shoulders.

→ Finish one set in this rhythm before bringing your left foot next to your right one and switching the position of the feet.

TIP **The combination of lunges and curls** results in a demanding exercise that challenges and trains your strength and coordination at the same time.

Let's stretch

FILL UP ON ENERGY

→ Stand at ease in front of an open window. Your legs are slightly apart, your knees slightly bent. If you want, you can close your eyes.

The test:

how's your fitness?

A victory isn't a victory unless you notice it. The following tests will help you to assess your current state of fitness and measure your progress. Carry out the test before you start your training program and repeat it after you've ended – you'll be happy with the results!

How fit are you?

1 Pushups – testing your arm strength

→ Try to do as many pushups as you can in 30 seconds. If you can't keep it up for the whole time, then count the pushups you're able to do correctly. You can do pushups in the classic position which is more demanding (see page 100), or support yourself on hands and knees.

Your score: how many pushups can you do?
1. 30 or more pushups (3 points)
2. 15 to 29 pushups (2 points)
3. 3 to 14 pushups (1 point)

2 Going for ripped abs

→ Lie on your back in front of a mirror, which is on the floor. Your feet are towards the mirror and your legs are bent. Press your heels into the floor and stretch your arms out beside your body.
→ Lift your head and shoulder blades far enough for you to see your eyes past your knees in the mirror.

Your score: How long can you look yourself in the eyes?
1. 40 or more seconds (3 points)
2. 20 to 39 seconds (2 points)
3. less than 20 seconds (1 point)

3 Test your stability

→ First stand up straight, with your feet apart at about shoulder width.

Your score: How flexible are you?
1. You can easily grasp your feet (3 points).
2. Your fingertips reach your toes (2 points).
3. Between your toes and your middle finger there's a space of at least a hand's length (1 point)

→ Now bend your knees until the thighs are horizontal. Hold this position.

Your score: How long can you hold it?
1. 30 seconds or more (3 points)
2. between 20 and 29 seconds (2 points)
3. less than 20 seconds (1 point)

4 Coordination: standing on one leg

→ Hold a watch in one hand or ask a training partner to time you.
→ You're standing upright with your eyes closed. Lift one leg slightly forward and trace a semi-circle in the air in front of you with the tip of your foot. While doing this do not straighten out your standing leg.

Your score: How long can you keep your balance?
1. over 20 seconds (3 points)
2. over 10 seconds (2 points)
3. less than 20 seconds (1 point)

5 What about your flexibility?

→ Sit up against a wall with your legs stretched forward. While exhaling bend over slowly. How far down your legs can you touch with your fingertips?
→ A light pulling sensation in the thighs is normal. But if there's pain then stop immediately. Note the position that you can hold for at least three seconds.

Credits

This edition published by
Barnes & Noble, Inc.,
by arrangement with
GRÄFE UND UNZER VERLAG GmbH

2004 Barnes & Noble Books

© 2004 GRÄFE UND UNZER VERLAG GmbH

M 10 9 8 7 6 5 4 3 2 1

ISBN 0-7607-60969

Production:
bookwise Medienproduktion GmbH, Munich

Translation:
José Medina, Munich

Printed in Singapore

Photo production: Christian Dahl
Other photos: Corbis: p. 4, 75; Andreas Hosch: pp. 86, 91; IFA: p. 22; Manfred Jahreiß: p. 82; Jump: front cover (top), pp. 1, 38, 102, 122; Mauritius: pp. 6, 8, 54, 114; Photonica: p. 2, back cover (centre); Tom Roch: pp. 31, 94; Reiner Schmitz: pp. 47, 51, 58, 62, 66, 67, 103, 106, 110, 111, 119; Stockfood: p. 55

Illustrations: Detlef Seidensticker

Acknowledgments:
The author wishes to give special thanks to Christine Wolters for her excellent editorial report on the text and her total support of his work on this book. Further thanks from the author and the publisher go to the adidas company in Herzogenaurach for its help in the preparation of the photo production of this book.

Important Notice:
All the advice, exercises and applications in this book were carefully researched by the author and were tested in practice. They are suitable for persons with a normal constitution. Nevertheless, it is all readers' own responsibility to decide whether, and how far, they can and wish to implement the suggestions in this book.
Neither the author nor the publisher can assume liability for any possible damage or injury resulting from the practical advice given in the book.